BAPTISM
OF *Love*

LEIF HETLAND

SONSHIP SERIES

Leif Hetland
P.O. Box 3049
Peachtree City, Georgia 30269
www.globalmissionawareness.com

www.burkhartbooks.com

Burkhart Books 2012
Bedford, Texas

This book is dedicated to my princess and first girl,
Laila Ann,
who is preparing to leave and cleave.

As a father,
I am very proud to have a daughter like you.
Love, Dad

"You are my beloved *daughter,*
in whom I am well pleased."

Matthew 3:17, NASB

Contents

Prologue

I studied Philosophy for several years of my life thoroughly and rigorously searching out what humanity had said, done, written, and sought. I gave myself completely to understanding the human psyche and the sociological reasons behind war, famine, and economic breakdown. I listened to the wise and gave ear to the foolish. I observed the rich and sat down with the poor. I gave money to the hungry and donated my clothes to the impoverished and orphaned. I never neglected the needy, never despised the widow, and offered a helping hand to anyone I could aid. After quite some time, I finally began to understand the tongue of humanity. Indeed, I had learned the language of mankind.

Not entirely satisfied with my accomplishments, I set out again on another quest. I began to pour myself into theology, mysticism, and the religions of the world, hoping to somehow earn the ability to understand the mysteries of 'God' and the knowledge of all that was Holy. I prayed, fasted, and spent endless hours reading, listening, and meditating on all those who were considered to be messengers of God. I listened to the prophets of religion, studied the magistrates of law, learned the words of the poets, sang the songs of the natives, repeated the liturgy of the priests, and practiced silence with the ascetics. After quite some time I finally began to understand the language of both men and angels. Indeed, I had learned to decipher the mysteries of ancient truths and celestial beings. When a person acted, I could discern his intentions. I could perceive untruth, unmask manipulation, and was quick to escape the puppeteering enticement that the ventriloquists of society often controlled the masses with. My mind was quick, my spirit strong, and my gift of prophecy was as direct and accurate as a skilled marksman. I accurately foretold of coming events, and I even healed many in the name of 'Faith'. I learned the power of the tongue, moving mountains, and driving the giants of doubt and unbelief into the sea. I learned the power of music, and trained myself to sing the songs of my fathers. The sound of my voice brought people to tears, joy, hope, and some to conversion. My life exuded brilliance, and I was anointed as a man of renown. Indeed, my life was like a fire, consuming all darkness around me with the flame of my 'God'.

Then one night, I heard a distant whisper, a whisper like none other. A whisper which passed through the spiralling galaxies of the heavens, through the twinkling stars and supernovas, through the majestic twilight of silver crescent moons, and the fiery flames of brilliant suns. A faint and kind whisper, delivered on the shoulders of a winter wind, softly spoke into my ear, "If you have not love then you are nothing." Prophecies will fail, the tongue will cease, and knowledge will vanish. Love never fails.

1 Corinthians 13

Chapter One

Immersed in Father God's Love

My greatest passion in life is to share the love of God with others, especially to those who have not yet heard the Gospel – the least, the last, and the lost. I believe that man's pursuit for happiness will end the moment he has an encounter with God's love. There is nothing like it in the world. It is too wonderful for me to express, and it is hard to explain how I truly feel when I meditate on His love for you and me. I was raised in a Christian home and I thought I knew God's love. The truth is, I had an idea of God's love, but I had never experienced it.

I am inspired to speak about God's love because I know there are only a few people in this world who truly understand what it means to be loved unconditionally. The rest have no idea what it is to receive and enjoy a love without strings attached, without preconditions, or without a prenuptial agreement. It is love that only our heavenly Father can give. I pray, as you read along, you will get to know Him and His amazing love.

Desperate Need

God's love is the answer to all our problems. As I have said in the past, if you have a revelation of a Big Daddy, then you will have small problems. If you perceive of God as your Small Daddy, then you will have big problems. The key, therefore, is to be aware of Father's big love for us.

We all need to know more about His great love. However, most of us have no idea where to begin. As I already mentioned, there are only a few people on this planet who are fortunate enough to have families who help them grasp the concept of unconditional love. For the rest of us, the idea is so foreign it is even difficult to imagine what unconditional love actually means. We have approximations of what the term "unconditional love" means, but we have never reached the point of assurance. We go on a quest to earn such love, but we fail miserably.

Love is often buried under the load of too many rules and expectations. I know how it feels to live in the kind of environment where the word "love" is used carelessly. I know what it means to live under the weight of high expectations and the constant pressure to live up to standards set by others. My earthly father is a wonderful person and a good husband to my mother. The whole time I lived with him, he demonstrated to our family that he was committed to us and that he was a good provider. But, no matter how great an earthly father

> *But I never reached the point where I knew God is not only in love with mankind, but also with me, Leif Hetland. I could not wrap my head around this idea. The short distance between a person's heart and mind can sometimes be a tricky chasm to traverse. I had all the right theology, but not the experience.*

we might have, through life's circumstances and situations, we will all be left with love deficits.

When I became a Christian, I was confronted with God's love. It is the central thesis of the Gospel message. God is love. He is so in love with the world, even in the midst of wickedness, and its people who are governed by sin. I accepted and believed, that indeed, God is love. But I never reached the point where I knew God is not only in love with mankind, but also with me, Leif Hetland. I could not wrap my head around this idea. The short distance between a person's heart and mind can sometimes be a tricky chasm to traverse. I had all the right theology, but not the experience.

My Baptism of Love

It was only through the Spirit of God that I was able to access His love for me. It was impossible to draw this kind of revelation from my personal experience. I could not extrapolate it using my intellect. True love came to me via supernatural means. It was an unearthly kind of love that was brought down from heaven and poured over my soul.

I remember every detail as if it happened yesterday. It was in the year 2000 when I went to a small gathering in Florida. Jack Taylor, my spiritual father, was there, as well as Dennis Jernigan, a world-renowned worship leader. Somebody prayed for me saying, *"I ask you, Holy Spirit, to come and take away anything in Leif's life that is not comfortable with love."* Then Dennis Jernigan began to sing a song, *Daddy's Song,* a love song about the love of Father God. Father's love connected with me through that song. The next thing I remember was being down on the floor. I was lying there like a child, and I was weeping. I could feel Father's love flowing over me. It was like liquid love going up and down my body, and in and out.

Before going to that meeting, I had thought I was motivated by love. I realized later on I was motivated by something else. I had gone to that meeting weighed down with many things going on in my life, my family, and my ministry. I was the president of an organization with representatives working in in many countries. I traveled all over the globe preaching and ministering to people. I was a husband and a father of four children, as well as a businessman. With so many responsibilities on my plate, intimacy with God was never a reality in my life. I was blindsided by the fact that I was doing so many things in my attempt to please God and people. During that period of my life, my wife and my children would probably tell you that my ministry was my mistress.

Yet, when I was in that meeting lying on the floor, the Lord performed a spiritual surgery in me. He transported me back to the time when I was twelve years old. I had been violated at that age and it was as if the Lord was telling me He knew what I had gone through. That night in Florida my loving Father wrapped His arms around me. I could feel

His presence and the powerful surge of His love flowing in me and through me. I was totally immersed in His pure love.

When I came home from that experience in Florida, my family instantly recognized the transformation. Not quite believing the change, they asked me, *"What has happened to you?"* My wife told me, *"You had the Baptism in the Spirit, and it was a powerful experience; signs and wonders came after that. But this Baptism of Love has changed you more than anything I have ever seen in your life."* Thank God for my wife. She helped me clarify what Father had done in me.

From that day forward, I knew I had to talk about that wonderful experience. At the same time, Father God began to increase my understanding of the type of baptism I had received. I realized that Jesus also had a similar experience. It was the reason Jesus was so effective in His ministry and was able to change the world. His power, wisdom, knowledge, and anointing was rooted in the assurance that His Daddy God would always love Him no matter what the circumstances. It gave Him the confidence, joy, peace, and resolve to carry the cross and die for the sins of all mankind. Now, here's the good news: Daddy God is willing to let you experience this same *Baptism of Love.*

You see, like Jesus, I had been baptized in water and the Holy Spirit. But Jesus experienced another baptism most of us have never heard of and that's the reason for this book.

The Secret

So often I see Christians, ministers and laymen alike, burnt out on Christianity, holy living, and the desire to be the Lord's hands and feet. Time after time I witness the haunting ghost of depression and the riddling cancer of bitterness consume a child of God with loneliness, failure, hopelessness, doubt, and feelings of abandonment. Fallen ministers, broken marriages, and schisms have spread like a pandemic throughout the church. It is not long before the old cliché question arises *"Where is the love?"* as in the case of Charles Stanley as written in his book *The Reason For My Hope, 1997:*

What happens to a person who knows about God's love only at the mind or intellectual level? Such a person has a theory but not an experience. A love void continues to exist, and over time, that void grows larger and becomes more frustrating. I believe that is especially true if a person is continuing to seek God and to desire all that God has for him or her.

Now, I didn't know that I was missing the love of God in my life. All I knew was that something was missing in my Christian experience. I would preach about the freedom that Christ gives, go home, look up to heaven, and say, "But what about me? Why don't I feel free?" I had an ache within me that I could not define or eliminate and, eventually, could not escape.

My Personal Encounter with God's Great Love

In intense inner pain and turmoil, I sought advice from four men whom I trusted explicitly. I called the men, who are people of the highest integrity, and I asked them to meet with me to hear me out with empathy and then to give me their wise counsel. I trusted God to help them to help me.

I met with the four men privately at a lodge in a wilderness area. I confessed to them that I was at the end of myself. I didn't know what to do. I didn't know where to go. I asked them if I could share with them my life and told them that after they had heard my story, I wanted them to give me their best advice. I assured them that I would do whatever they advised me to do. I had that much respect for them. I also conveyed to them how desperate I was and how extremely serious I was about receiving their help. They generously agreed to hear me out and to be God's instruments in my life.

I talked all afternoon and evening. I woke up several times in the middle of the night and wrote a total of seventeen pages in longhand— legal-sized pages—of things I wanted to be sure to tell them the next morning. I told them everything I remembered about my early life and all the

For the first time in my life, I felt emotionally that God loved me. I had known as a fact from His Word that God loved me. I had believed by faith that God loved me. I had accepted the fact that love is God's nature. But until that day, not very many years ago, I had never emotionally felt God loving me.

17

highlights—both painful and positive—of my adult life and ministry. When I was finished—and believe me, I was completely spent at that point-—I said, "Now, whatever you tell me to do, I'll do it."

They asked me two or three questions, and then one of the men who was sitting directly across the table from me said, "Charles, put your head on the table and close your eyes." I did. He said to me very kindly, "Charles, I want you to envision your father picking you up in his arms and holding you." After a few moments, he said, "What do you feel?"

I burst out crying. And I cried and I cried and I cried. I could not stop crying. Finally, when I stopped, he asked me again, "What do you feel?" I said, "I feel warm, loved, secure. I feel good." And I started weeping again.

For the first time in my life, I felt emotionally that God loved me. I had known as a fact from His Word that God loved me. I had believed by faith that God loved me. I had accepted the fact that love is God's nature. But until that day, not very many years ago, I had never emotionally felt God loving me.

God used that encounter with those four men, and that one simple question, to unlock the love void in my life and to begin to pour into it a flood of His divine love.

The full release of God's love didn't happen in a day. It was a process, little by little. But the more I explored the love of God, the more God began to reveal my true identity in Christ—that I belonged to Him as I had never belonged to anybody, that I was worth something to Him, and that He loved me beyond measure. I discovered that when I got to the end of myself and all of my efforts at striving for perfection, a kind and gracious heavenly Father who had loved me unconditionally all my life. Let me assure you, nothing is more liberating than that discovery.

There is no end to God's love, and there ultimately will be no end to our ability to experience it. We need never have love-starved hearts again. His desire is to overflow us with His love and, all the while, to enlarge our capacity to experience His love and give it to others.

The more I experienced God's love, the more I began to understand the importance of saying to others, "God loves you just the way you are." I came to be able to love others as they were and to be far less critical of their failed efforts or lack of perfection. God's love for me became the source of a great love for others. The outpouring of God's love into my life positively affected my ministry and my relationships with others. I had been invaded by love, and I couldn't keep it to myself.

From that day in the mountains, I had a sense of inner closeness with God that I had never experienced before. I knew I could trust Him regardless of what happened to me, regardless of any mistakes I might make, regardless of how I might respond or react in my humanity. I had a strong feeling of assurance that I had always been loved, was loved now, and would always be loved with a vast love that was beyond my comprehension, but that I could experience nonetheless on a daily basis.

Once intimacy with God has been established, it grows. There is no end to God's love, and there ultimately will be no end to our ability to experience it. We need never have love-starved hearts again. His desire is to overflow us with His love and, all the while, to enlarge our capacity to experience His love and give it to others.

I came to the place where I could say with the apostle John, "I have known the love of God. I believe the love of God."

In John 15, Jesus reveals to us another facet of abundant living. This revelation is a vital key to living a life of ministry wherein we never burn out, rust out, or fall into the shambles of a broken inner life. In this incredible snippet from the text of John, Jesus speaks to us a life-transforming string of words, *"Love one another as I have loved you."* This statement is so often passed over, or shuffled together, alongside the usual verses pertaining to God's love. Yet, we must not miss the magnitude of what Jesus is really saying here. Jesus is teaching us that our souls are like a well. His love is the only liquid that can fill us. The world so often comes to drink from our wells, and instead of receiving the bubbling fountain of fresh living water that Jesus offers, they instead receive the stale and stagnate liquid of our own lukewarm theology. The world is not looking for a doctrine: they are looking for love, the love of our Father manifested to them in human form. This is why John urges us in 1 John 4 by saying, *"No one has ever seen God; but if we love one another, God lives in us and His love is made complete in us."* Without love it is impossible to see God. When we love we literally open up blind souls and reveal the Living God to them.

Oh the power of Father's Love! The living water of divine love opens the eyes of the lost, searching, rejected, and wounded, sustaining them with the heavenly fountain of eternal compassion! No one has seen God, yet they see Him in the eyes of a son or daughter that loves.

Never have I witnessed the effects of love transforming an environment like I have in Pakistan. I have ventured into some of the darkest areas in Pakistan, where Light has never gone before. On numerous occasions standing in one of our Peace Conferences giving a talk as a son, I can release the love of heaven and watch an entire atmosphere transform. Those who have accompanied me on these trips are a witness to this.

I am now referred to as the *Ambassador of Love* in Pakistan. I have been going to Pakistan now for many years. On a recent trip to Pakistan I was introduced as an *Ambassador of Love* in various settings, including GMA's Annual Peace Conference. Several hundred well-known government and religious leaders attend this conference. It is an honor to represent the Kingdom of God in such a manner. Before my *Baptism of Love* I know I could never

It is not only illogical, but also entirely absurd to imagine producing something without first receiving the materials necessary for it!

21

have been entrusted with this assignment.

God is love and apart from Him we are capable of doing nothing good – much less, loving broken people. Here is the secret; we cannot love others beyond the capacity that we have allowed God to love us. *Our love comes from His love.* We will burn out, rust out, and give up if we seek to love from our own strength and resources. We can only love others as Christ loves us. We do not need more books, doctrinal dissertations, or catchy songs. We need a *Baptism of Love!*

The Samaritan woman at the well displays such a beautiful depiction of the world as it comes to Christ. She ends up leaving her water pot by the well! She has been filled with the living water of Father God's love! So often the precious sons and daughters of God try to love, give, and heal, when they themselves have not received such from their Father in heaven. I have done it myself and, from personal testimony, I can say with authority that it will drain dry the well of your soul, leaving you with an empty and disillusioned heart. We must be baptized with the power of God's love and love the world from that place. It is not only illogical, but also entirely absurd to imagine *producing* something without first receiving the materials necessary for it! Likewise, we cannot produce the healing love of the Father without first receiving it! If we have not been baptized in God's love, if we have not first received God's love, then we cannot release it. Period. Our love is the product of His love. This is the only way we can communicate the love of our Father in the face of a world overflowing with brokenness, war, and persecution.

Before we can love a hate filled world, heal the wounded masses, kiss the leper, cherish the widow, protect the orphan, or give life to the dying, we, ourselves, must first be loved by the God of love. We cannot baptize the world in rivers of living water, nor quench the thirst of parched tongues, if we ourselves have not been submerged and regenerated in the raging waters of everlasting compassion and mercy! Love never fails, and we will never fail if love has prevailed over us! ✝This is the secret—Love one another as the Father loves you!

Chapter Two

Three Kinds of Baptisms

John the Baptist selected a strategic spot in which to preach. He probably chose a ford in the Jordan River, a place shallow enough for people to cross. In addition to those who wanted to go to the other side of the river, there were those who came near to fetch water. A few more came to fish. There were also small boats which transported people and goods, moving precious cargo across Israel because the river was the easiest way to travel from Mount Hermon in the north towards the Dead Sea in the south, and vice versa. In other words, John chose the best place to draw a crowd. It was also an ideal location because those receiving the message of John the Baptist had to demonstrate obedience and commitment to the Lord through water baptism.

Baptizing people in the Jordan River was also a powerful teaching tool to help them understand the nature of baptism. The flowing stream was a testament to the purposeful effect of baptism, and the need for the element of water to come in contact with the repentant sinners to sweep away the grime and dirt from their person. When the new believer waded into the river, he was totally surrounded by water, and as his body felt the pulsating power of the river he experienced the after-effect of baptism, which is a changed life. As most Christians have experienced, the person who comes out of the water is not the same person who was immersed into it. This is what we call the born-again experience.

For many weeks John the Baptist was a familiar sight in that particular area of the Jordan River. He declared, *"The Kingdom of God is at hand."* Crowds would gather because they were hungry for God's word. For the previous four hundred years, no one had been sent to speak on behalf of the Lord of the heavens. But listening to John, they knew the dry spell was about to be broken. Therefore, the hearers realized the need to repent and be baptized.

John preached against the sins of Israel and the need to be under submission to the coming King. However, one day John was astounded as he saw Jesus coming. John would later explain that he himself was simply a water baptizer, and the element of water was a mere symbol of repentance, an outward symbolism of an inward experience. He further proclaimed that Jesus was the one who would baptize with fire.

Jesus convinced John it was for righteousness sake that the Son of God must submit to the ministry of the forerunner. John consented and the Apostle Matthew recounted the details of the event:

> *"As soon as Jesus was baptized, he went up out of the water. At that moment heaven was opened, and he saw the Spirit of God descending like a dove and lighting on him. And a voice from heaven said, 'This is my Son, whom I love; with him I am well pleased.'"*

> Matthew 3:16-17, NIV

By studying this pivotal moment in human history, we learn more about Jesus' life and ministry and the reason He was able to make such an impact. It is also important to understand the nature of baptism. As we take a closer look at Jesus' *Baptism of Love*, we must have a common understanding when we talk about the expected outcome of coming under that special outpouring from the Father.

Baptism of Water

Let us, therefore, pay careful attention to three key aspects of this momentous event before Jesus launched His ministry. First, Jesus was immersed in water (upward experience). Secondly, Jesus was immersed in the Holy Spirit (outward experience), and thirdly, Jesus was immersed in His Father's love (inward experience).

Let us take a look at the first aspect. The Bible says that Jesus came up out of the water. This means that Jesus did not merely wash His body, arms, and legs mimicking the activities of the temple priests. Yes, He used the river water for cleansing, but in that moment He was completely immersed into it. The action was reminiscent of what the prophet Elisha instructed General Naaman of the Assyrian army to do when he told Naaman to take a dip in the Jordan River as an act of obedience and commitment to Yahweh. This resulted in the healing of Naaman's infirmity. Bible scholars also assert that baptism comes from the ancient term *"baptize,"* usually illustrated as the action of immersing a piece of cloth into a dye bath.

Baptism of water is a symbolic act of what has taken place in our lives (salvation). When we repent of our sins, the blood of Jesus washes us clean. Baptism of water signifies an upward experience of being reconciled with our heavenly Father.

Baptism of the Holy Spirit

Secondly, the Spirit of God came down from heaven and descended upon Jesus. This is the first time in the Bible where we can see the Holy Spirit become closely associated with a person outside the context of rigorous religious standards such as the regulations connected with the Jewish temple. In the Old Testament, the Spirit of God evoked a feeling of dread rather than love. The manifestation of the Spirit brought terror to the hearts of the ancients because they tried to draw near on the basis of their perceived goodness and abilities through the observance of the Law.

It was only the High Priest who could enter into the Presence of God and be engulfed with the power from on high and the Spirit of a *Holy, Holy, Holy* God. Only the High Priest was allowed to have fellowship with God face-to-face, and only then by adhering to an exacting standard of purification—cleansing the physical and spiritual body with water and dealing with his sins using animal sacrifices. Furthermore, he could only enjoy this privilege once a year.

We can understand the amazement of John the Baptist when he saw the Holy Spirit through the gift of spiritual vision. He described it as having the characteristics of a meek bird coming down slowly and gently on top of Jesus and forever dwelling with the Son of God. We also have to understand that the Spirit did not only abide with Christ, but the Bible also says that Jesus was filled with the Holy Spirit in *full measure*. The Holy Spirit was not only above Him, the Spirit was with Him wherever He went; and the Holy Spirit was in Him. In other words, the Spirit surrounded Jesus and flowed through Christ. This explains why Jesus called this experience *"the Baptism with the Holy Spirit."* (see Acts 1:5)

I have heard Bill Johnson say, *"The Holy Spirit is in us for our sake, and on us for others sake."* Jesus went into the water with the Holy Spirit in Him. He came out of the water with the Holy Spirit on Him. Before this time, Jesus had not done any miracles. He needed the Holy Spirit on Him to accomplish His assignment and release the Kingdom of God to others.

> *If Satan can get us to doubt our identity as sons and daughters of Father God, then we will continuously strive for approval and acceptance and operate out of a position of servantship instead of Sonship. Servants work for a paycheck. Sons receive inheritance.*

These two forms of baptism—the baptism of water and of the Holy Spirit—were expounded to show forth the nature of baptism, which is immersion. This is imperative because when we get to the discussion regarding the *Baptism of Love*, the image of a person covered from head to toe with the element of baptism is the picture we need to keep in mind.

Baptism of Love

Now, let us look at the third aspect of the event and we can immediately sense a major difference. There were no visible signs seen except the words the Father spoke to Jesus. This is the reason many people miss this important part of the story. John the Baptist and his disciples heard the same voice. Father God was pleased to announce to those who were able to listen that this was His Son whom He loved and in whom He was well pleased. The thundering voice of the Father equaled what He felt—He was overjoyed and full of love just looking at His Son, Jesus Christ.

Just like the water and the Spirit baptism that came before, the Father's love enveloped Jesus and covered Him from within and without. The Father's love overwhelmed Jesus and flooded His inner being.

Jesus' test in the wilderness following His three baptisms was a test of *Sonship*. Jesus, as a man, needed the affirmation of His Father. Father God said, *"This is my beloved son whom I am well pleased with."* Jesus had an A+ on His report card before He entered the test of the wilderness, performed any miracle, preached any sermon or had any following. It had nothing to do with what He did, but who He was and Whose He was.

What was the first thing Satan hit him with when He entered the wilderness, *"**IF** you are the **son** of God?"* Like Jesus we must pass the test of *Sonship* in order to be entrusted with the supernatural and release the Kingdom of God here on earth. If Satan can get us to doubt our identity as sons and daughters of Father God, then we will continuously strive for approval and acceptance and operate out of a position of servant-ship instead of *Sonship*. Servants work for a paycheck. Sons receive inheritance.

The Importance of Being Born-Again, Living in the Holy Spirit, and Walking in Father God's Love

Baptism is immersion, and so we need to ask, *"Immersion into what?"* It is immersion into a particular gift—a gift that comes from our Father God. It is not only an immersion, but an action similar to a fabric designer immersing a piece of cloth into a dye bath hoping to transform an ordinary piece of cloth into something beautiful and useful. Baptism means to be covered completely, and to absorb what Father wants to give, thus moving one from glory to glory. His goal is to fill us and surround us with His goodness, mercy, grace, and love.

In the first level of baptism, we need to be immersed into the gift of salvation and righteousness. The Bible says that we receive righteousness through faith. In the same way that Abraham was justified through faith, we too must receive the forgiveness of sin and salvation as a gift and not as a right that we demand based on our abilities and accomplishments.

When we go through the Baptism of Water, we receive the gift of righteousness. We are cleansed not through our own personal standard of holiness or merit. The Word of God is crystal clear in this regard. It asserts, *"For it is by grace you have been saved, through faith—and this not from yourselves, it is the gift of God— not by works, so that no one can boast."* (Ephesians 2:8-9, NIV) It is, indeed, a gift from our Father.

The second level of experience is an immersion into the gift of power through the Holy Spirit (Acts 1:4). Jesus said, *"But you will receive power when the Holy Spirit comes on you…"* (Acts 1:8, NIV) How many Christians operate in ministry having no access to the gift of the Holy Spirit? The Apostle Paul said there are people "…holding to a form of godliness, although they have denied its power." (2 Timothy 3:5, NIV) We can't afford to challenge demonic forces and challenge the carnality of the world without the supernatural gift that comes from God. But even if we can access the supernatural realm and can stand with confidence in the righteousness of new life, the burden and the pressure of Christian life and ministry can push us to the breaking point if we don't have complete access to what has been prepared for us.

The third gift, the *Baptism of Love*, is also a gift that we need to receive because it will keep us afloat in times of testing and trials. How many servants of God have started a ministry ablaze with the passion to conquer the world, only to fall by the wayside unable to stand back to their feet after they get hit with a low blow from the enemy? Are you going to follow the same path? It can be avoided by an experience with your Father's love.

I can so identify with Charles Finney's story as told on Carl Thomas.net:

Within hours of his receiving saving grace he had a powerful encounter with the love of God. This infilling empowered him and propelled him to be among the great revivalists of all time. Finney set a whole section of our country on fire for Jesus in the early 19th century. Here is his account of his encounter with God the afternoon of his conversion.

There was no fire, and no light, in the room; nevertheless it appeared to me as if it were perfectly light. As I went in and shut the door after me, it seemed as if I met the Lord Jesus Christ face to face. It did not occur to me then, nor did it for some time afterward, that it was wholly a mental state. On the contrary it seemed to me that I saw him as I would see any other man. He said nothing, but looked at me in such a manner as to break me right down at his feet. I have always since regarded this as a most remarkable state of mind; for it seemed to me a reality, that he stood before me, and I fell down at his feet and poured out my soul to him. I wept aloud like a child, and made such confessions as I could with my choked utterance. It seemed to me that I bathed his feet with my tears; and yet I had no distinct impression that I touched him, that I recollect.

I must have continued in this state for a good while; but my mind was too much absorbed with the interview to recollect anything that I said. But I know, as soon as my mind became calm enough to break off from the interview, I returned to the front office, and found that the fire that I had made of large wood was nearly burned out. But as I turned and was about to take a seat by the fire, I received a mighty baptism of the Holy Ghost. Without any expectation of it, without ever having the thought in my mind that there was any such thing for me, without any recollection that I had ever heard the thing mentioned by any person in the world, the Holy Spirit descended upon me in a manner that seemed to go through my body and soul. I could feel the impression, like a wave of electricity, going through and through me.

Indeed it seemed to come in waves and waves of liquid love, for I could not express it in any other way. It seemed like the very breath of God. I can recollect distinctly that it seemed to fan me, like immense wings.

> *No words can express the wonderful love that was shed abroad in my heart. I wept aloud with joy and love; and I do not know but I should say, I literally bellowed out unutterable gushings of my heart. These waves came over me, and over me, and over me, one after the other, until I recollect I cried out, "I shall die if these wavers continue to pass over me." I said, "Lord, I cannot bear any more;" yet I had no fear of death.*

Jesus' baptism of His Father's love was simply an affirmation of what is and was true for all of eternity, *"In the beginning was the Word and the Word was with God and the Word was God."* (John 1:1, NIV) The Father loved the Son even before time began. But in our case, our *Baptism of Love* is a gift from our Father. This is because there is nothing in us that deserves this form of baptism. In fact, many of us

> **But God's love for us is not based on feelings; it is based on a decision. It is a gift given to those who are not worthy of such love.**

do not expect this kind of attention, nor are we aware that we can receive this lavish gift from above.

We usually define love as an emotion. We assume we love if we feel good, and we don't love if we feel rotten. But God's love for us is not based on feelings; it is based on a decision. It is a gift given to those who are not worthy of such love. It is like the love of Boaz for Ruth. Boaz was a free man and a powerful leader; no one could have forced him to love a widow. And yet he did. It is like the love of the father towards his prodigal son. The father was never legally bound to give shelter and provision to a wicked and rebellious son. And yet he did. He even gave more by restoring him to a position of honor and privilege.

We need the righteousness that comes from being born again. This is powerfully illustrated by the Baptism in Water, as we die to our former self and the remains of that sinful past is buried in a watery grave. We need righteousness to be the salt and light of the world. If we are as corrupt as the rest of mankind, then, as Christians, we lose our purpose and no longer have the ability to be used by God. Men will trample upon the salt that has lost its flavor. In other words, it has no ability to influence the world and transform it.

While we need the baptism of repentance, we also need the power of the Spirit. It is the power that comes from above that can give life to our words. It is the power that quickens the soul and ignites the fire of ministry. But more importantly we need love. It is love that causes us to walk the extra mile, turn the other cheek, and become agents of reconciliation, peacemakers, history makers, lovers of God and people. We need all three baptisms, especially the third one that we tend to ignore and know less about.

The Secret to Success—the Jesus Way

We have identified the key aspects of Jesus' baptism by John. But we need to ask the question, "Why are Christians only aware of two and not three forms of baptism?" This can be partially explained by studying the testimony of John the Baptist who said that he was sent to baptize with water, but Jesus came to baptize with fire. Christians tend to focus on these two baptisms because of the way John emphasized it. We can easily envision this scene: the Jordan River as a backdrop and in the foreground Jesus and the Holy Spirit. These images dominate the baptism story and, thus, are easily remembered by Christians. This is the reason we concentrate our attention on these two baptisms (water and the Spirit) and neglect the third.

Jesus validated John's testimony regarding Water Baptism and Baptism in the Holy Spirit when He said, *"For John baptized with water, but in a few days you will be baptized with the Holy Spirit."* (Acts 1:5, NIV) Now, we know why we give priority to these two forms of baptisms, for these were emphasized in the initial encounter. On the other hand, it must be made clear that Jesus spent more time and energy talking about love than talking about spiritual cleansing and spiritual power. Love is the first requirement in order to succeed in life and in ministry (see 1 Corinthians 13:1-3). Even Jesus would have found it impossible to live a life of holiness and power without the *Baptism of Love*.

He needed more than the assurance that He was righteous. He needed more than anointing to go through with the ordeal of crucifixion. Even if He possessed superhuman strength, it would have been impossible for Jesus to go through all of these without first having the necessary assurance—the assurance that He was loved completely and unconditionally.

I believe it would have been impossible for Jesus to endure the demonic and physical attacks hurled at Him during His three and a half years of ministry without His Father's outpouring of love that day in the Jordan River. I believe Jesus needed more than integrity and power to defeat the devil when He faced-off with Satan in the wilderness. He needed more than the assurance that He was righteous. He needed more than anointing to go through with the ordeal of crucifixion. Even if He possessed superhuman strength, it would have been impossible for Jesus to go through all of these without first having the necessary assurance—the assurance that He was loved completely and unconditionally.

The simple truth is—our Father in Heaven loves us with an unconditional love that cannot be stopped. So often I see men and women working, striving, and wearing themselves out trying to acquire God's love. So often we walk the 'Christian' path backwards. We spend the bulk of our lives tortured on the 'Cross' asking, *"Why has thou forsaken me?"* We then move to the 'Garden of Gethsemane' where we feel imprisoned by those who were closest to us, and after a long hard life of sick people and demonic activity, we come to the place where we realize that our righteousness was

> *The event of Christ's baptism in scripture screams volumes to us concerning what is important in heaven's eyes. Father accepted Jesus, the perfect Son, long before Jesus took on the Cross.*

all just 'filthy rags'. Our Father in Heaven wishes to save us from such methodology.

In Jesus, who is the perfect image of His Father, not the Father, we see that the first act of 'Righteousness' is simply the revelation and reception of Abba's love. Without the Baptism of God's love, there will be no strength to walk the walk of Faith. Orphans live *for* love, sons live *from* love. The event of Christ's baptism in scripture screams volumes to us concerning what is important in heaven's eyes. Father accepted Jesus, the perfect Son, long before Jesus took on the Cross. We must understand that no one can accomplish the death of the cross without first receiving the life giving Baptism of Papa's love. As gasoline fuels a car, so God's love fuels us. As sons and daughters of God, we must open our lives to the reality of the Father and understand that our accomplishments merit us nothing.

We need the same experience. We need all three baptisms, but more importantly we need to know first hand that the Father loves us without pre-conditions. However, we can easily gravitate to power and not to love. We want the ability to accomplish things – to build, plant, and influence the outcome of human history; but we are unaware that love is the key. Love is the locomotive that pulls everything through, and puts everything in place.

Love sometimes can't be seen, only felt; but such a wonderful thing is God's love. His love makes everything possible. Fear is gone the moment love comes in. Peace is a mere by-product of His steadfast love, because peace comes when we are assured of protection day and night. Joy is the result of knowing that we belong to Someone who will never leave us nor forsake us. Jesus succeeded in ministry and in His personal life, because He had the assurance of His Father's love. It is time for us to partake of the same, because this outpouring of love is available to those who call God their Father.

Living as the Beloved

Long before Jesus ever preached the gospel, healed the sick, raised the dead or died and rose again, He was baptized in love and knew His identity as a son. It is simply profound that Christ came to earth specifically to be the propitiation for the sins of humanity on the cross. Yet, long before He accomplished His divine mission, His Father accepted him. Father approved Jesus of Nazareth, who is the sacrificial Lamb of God, long before He ever fulfilled His assignment! He was first in total alignment with His Father, which resulted in Him completing His assignment. When John the Baptist baptized Jesus the skies split, a dove descended (and never ascended), and a voice resounded, *"This is my beloved Son with whom I am well pleased."* You and I, just as Jesus, have been given Father's stamp of approval long before we ever accomplished anything in this life. You are His beloved, so, ***be loved.***

Chapter Three

The Revelation of Longing

Jesus said Father so loved the world that He gave His one and only Son to die for our sins so that whoever believes in Him will never perish but have eternal life. This statement spoken long before His crucifixion is like Isaac asking Abraham where the sacrifice was– a gut-wrenching statement foretold by the one who was about to be offered up for the sin of the world. This is the extent of our Father's love for us. Is there any good thing He will withhold from us? Is He withholding the wonderful experience that comes from being baptized in His love? The Word of God has a quick answer for this question, *"He who did not spare his own Son, but gave Him up for us all—how will He not also, along with Him, graciously give us all things?"* (Romans 8:32) You have no idea how much God is longing to be near you, to embrace you, and to be a Father to you. He is ready to bestow if you are ready to grow in His love.

The key to receiving this gift is to understand that Jesus has paved the way for us. *"For those God foreknew He also predestined to be conformed to the likeness of His Son, that He might be the firstborn among many brothers."* (Romans 8:29) Jesus is the Way; so we ought to follow. Jesus is the tailor's master-pattern; so we need to copy. Jesus is the potter's master-mold; so we need to conform. We are co-heirs with Christ, and Christ is in us. Let us not be ignorant of what rightfully belongs to us as heirs because the Son has paved the way. But first we need to re-discover what Jesus received that fateful day in the Jordan River. As you dig deeper, you will be amazed at what is in store for *you*.

The Revelation of our Father's Heart

Before going any further, it is important to be doubly blessed from the knowledge that there are two versions of Jesus' baptism in the Jordan River. The first version can be seen in the account of Matthew. The second account is found in the book of John, who recorded the event from the perspective of an eyewitness. Both disciples saw the manifestation of baptism, and they witnessed Father's connection with Jesus that day. Matthew's account tells us that John the Baptist (and probably his disciples) heard the Father proclaim His love for Jesus saying, *"And a voice from heaven said, 'This is my Son, whom I love; with Him I am well pleased.'"* (Matthew 3:17, NIV)

John the Beloved corroborated this eyewitness account. In his gospel, John recorded the testimony of the Baptizer who said the Father spoke the moment the Holy Spirit alighted on Jesus (see John 1:33). Father could not hide His excitement, and He wanted the world to know about this *Baptism of Love*.

This second version is also recounted in both the gospels of Mark and Luke. They both describe the event from the perspective of Jesus, who was not only aware of the good things His Father declared in the presence of many, but He also experienced a personal revelation of His Father's love for Himself. Therefore, at the exact moment His Father made a public announcement of love and affirmation, He also whispered an intimate message to the ears of His one and only, *"You are my Son whom I love; with You I am well pleased."* (Mark 1:11; Luke 3:22)

You can just imagine the impact these words of affirmation had on the life and ministry of the Lord. He had the full support of his Daddy God. Thus, He walked on water, passed through an angry mob unscathed, received provisions in

We have to understand that the Son of God left power and majesty in heaven when He decided to come in the form of human flesh. Therefore, everything He did in three and a half years of ministry was all accomplished through the power of the Holy Spirit and the power of His Father's love flowing through His innermost being.

times of need, experienced supernatural favor, and lived the life of an overcomer. He did this not because He was powerful and almighty in himself, but because He had a Big Daddy working on His behalf.

We have to understand that the Son of God left power and majesty in heaven when He decided to come in the form of human flesh. Therefore, everything He did in three and a half years of ministry was all accomplished through the power of the Holy Spirit and the power of His Father's love flowing through His innermost being.

The Yearning of our Father

Jesus' *Baptism of Love* was more than an emotional event; it was a revelation of a Father's heart towards His Son. Father God made three short, but sweet declarations. Firstly, He made an emphatic statement: I am Father and you are my Son. Secondly, He clarified the context of the Father-Son relationship: I love you. Finally, He made the ultimate assurance that this love is unconditional when He said: In You I am well pleased.

In the following chapter we will take a closer look at these three statements, which contain revelations from our Father's heart. However, in this section, let us simply focus on the first thing the Father declared when the Spirit alighted on Jesus, embraced Him, and covered Him with love just like the waters cover the sea. The first statement was filled with words of affection and longing, *"You are my Son."* These are tender words Father would also love you to receive.

Your Father Yearns to be Close to You

When my first child was born, I could not believe what I felt. Nothing had prepared me for the exhilaration of being a dad. I lifted my baby in my arms and struggled to find the words to express to this cute little thing how happy I was. As I stood there in the hospital nursery, I could not make myself leave. If not for the time constraints, I would have gladly stayed there the whole night watching. I longed to be there close to my baby. I could not wait to bring that precious little bundle of joy home. My heart was entwined with that of my little darling.

Father God felt the same way every time He laid eyes on Jesus, but, on that day at the Jordan, He had to make an announcement. God needed to confirm the identity of the Son-God to prove to the world that Jesus of Nazareth was no ordinary person, and that, indeed, Jesus was the Lord and Savior of the world. The Father's statement will reverberate all over the planet and down through the ages. It was not only John the Baptist nor his disciples who waited with bated breath to hear what God was saying regarding Jesus. The devil was also there waiting eagerly to know the detailed description of the true identity of the Son of Man.

Jesus' Father could have said many things. He could have said, *"This is Jesus the King of kings; bow down and worship Him."* He could have also said, *"This is Jesus the Word of God made flesh; obey His every word and you will be saved."* He could have said, *"This is Jesus, the Anointed One; you can approach Him if you need healing."*

Father could have chosen any of those lines to introduce

> *The worship of the people paled in comparison to what the Father felt inside. He simply wanted to celebrate the fact that Jesus was His Son and that He was so happy to be near Him...the whole universe had nothing to offer which would distract Him from what He considered the most beautiful and most important person in heaven and on earth—His eye was upon Jesus, His one and only son.*

His son to the world. But instead He made a deliberate decision to say, *"This is my Son."* The titles and the accolades meant nothing at that specific point in time. The worship of the people paled in comparison to what His Father felt inside. He simply wanted to celebrate the fact that Jesus was His Son and that He was so happy to be near Him. From the vantage point of Father, the whole universe had nothing to offer which would distract Him from what He considered the most beautiful and most important person in heaven and on earth—His eye was upon Jesus, His one and only son.

Now a person can argue that Father God loves Jesus simply because He has no sin and because He is the Son of God. Father God also loves you so much that He gave His Son as an offering to pay for your sins. You must understand that Father God loves you just as much as He loves Jesus. If you've received Jesus into your life, then every time your Father sees you, He no longer sees the old sinner and old rebel. He sees His Son in you. Just as in the Jordan River baptism, Father will also say to you, *"You are my child. I love you and I am well pleased with you."*

Your Father Yearns to Reveal the Real You

The Father not only longs to be with you but He also longs to reveal your true identity and true value. The world has succeeded in distorting the way you see your own self-image. Movies, television programs and commercials, magazines, and even social networking sites, keep the pressure building, telling you that you are not good enough. They encourage you to compare your wealth and abilities to other people. They say they are successful while you are not. The Father sees the effect this has on you, and He does not want to wait a second longer. He wants to set you free with the truth of His unconditional love. He wants you to have life to the full without unnecessary burdens to carry. He wants you to be liberated with the knowledge that you were created as an object of His love. This is why He longs to reveal the real you.

The first step is to secure the proper ID. We need an accurate identification of who we really are. Let me give you an illustration. There is no way you can barge into the corporate offices of top companies like Google, Microsoft, or General Motors without the proper identification. Their security personnel will promptly escort you out. Thus, no one is foolish enough to waste time attempting to enter these places without authorization or the credentials needed to talk face-to-face with the CEO. However, what if you have the proper ID and never know you have the power to walk into the boardroom and demand their attention?

What if your whole life you are told that you are a pauper or an illegitimate child, but, in truth, you are the long lost child of a multi-billionaire? What if your dad is the owner of a lucrative business, but you were separated from birth and, therefore, you have no clue as to the things that are available to you? You are the legal heir, and it is your birthright to take command of the enterprise, but what is keeping you from assuming control is the lack of self-knowledge. Your lost identity could be a case of mistaken identity if the people around you do not perceive your true value and whenever they see you they simply dismiss you as insignificant.

When your true identity is revealed, then everything will change. You suddenly have access to the business empire built by your dad, and your life will never be the same. This is an exciting tale—from a pauper to a prince—in the twinkling of an eye.

Unfortunately, in this situation, you are believing a lie. Many years have passed and the lie has become ingrained as truth in your heart and mind. You have completely embraced the false identity that you are an orphan when, in truth, you are an heir to a business empire. So you simply drift from place to place with no direction in life and wait for life to end, like a jelly fish washed ashore resigned to its fate. But, ironically, this is not who you are. You are actually the child of a great being and you simply have to be reconnected with your father and have your true identity revealed.

When your true identity is revealed, then everything will change. You suddenly have access to the business empire built by your dad, and your life will never be the same. This is an exciting tale – from a pauper to a prince – in the twinkling of an eye. However, the Bible has a much better story to tell:

> "...when we were God's enemies, we were reconciled to him through the death of his Son, how much more, having been reconciled, shall we be saved through his life! Not only is this so, but we also rejoice in God through our Lord Jesus Christ, through whom we have now received reconciliation."
>
> Romans 5:10, NIV

You can be a Bible-believing Christian without any idea that you have a good Father in heaven and that you have access to everything He owns. Jesus was never ignorant of His true identity, because He received a *Baptism of Love* from Father God. He, therefore, lived a productive and victorious life.

51

Jesus commanded the storm to cease, the fig tree to wither, the demons to flee, the pain to go away, the dead to rise, and demonstrated authority over the natural and physical realm, not because He was powerful in Himself, but simply because He had the correct ID. In the Jordan River, He received the absolute commendation from the Father, *"This is my Son!"*

I can't contain my excitement thinking about the day when more and more of God's children will receive a touch from their Father which will cause them to re-adjust their idea of "self." For thousands of years, too many have been content to wallow in self-pity, unable to defeat the devil and impact their communities. I get so excited thinking about the promise of our Father that Jesus is our role model, the perfect example, and the showcase of things to come. Jesus received the revelation that the Father longed to be with Him and to reveal His true identity. The Bible says this privilege is available to *all* those who believe (see John 1:12). This means that God is more than willing to do for us just what He did for His son Jesus.

God Longs to be Your Father

It is sometimes crazy to think that God, the omniscient and omnipotent One, is in love with you. But this is the truth, and you simply need to get used to it. If He had a tree, He would carve your name in it. If He had a refrigerator, your picture would be on it. If He had a wallet, your picture would be in it. He does things to show His love, and, most of the time, we are unaware. The sunrise is faithful every day, and the sunset the same. The rain comes to give us drink. Air is free. God sends us these love notes. We keep ignoring them, but He persists.

> *The sunrise is faithful every day, and the sunset the same. The rain comes to give us drink. Air is free. God sends us these love notes. We keep ignoring them, but He persists.*

Our Lord in heaven has one desire; He longs to be a Father to you. I have four children; I cannot begin to tell you how much I want to be a father to them. Sometimes they don't want me to father them, but my desire does not fade away simply because there are bumps in the road and things do not go my way. I continue to seek them and to find ways to father them. If I have that kind of commitment to my children while I am an imperfect human being, you can just imagine the deep longing in the heart of God to be a Father to you.

Your Father longs to be with you. He is yearning to be your Daddy, to be a helping hand, a guide, a mentor, a strong arm of protection, and yet to be gentle enough to be approachable. He wants to be all these things and more. Those who have already received this revelation are in agreement. This is not a new thing. In the Book of Beginnings we are told the original plan of our Father. His original intention was to dote on sons and daughters who were originally conformed to His image. This is still His heart today. As in the case of my spiritual son, Paul Yadao:

May 2006 marked a major turning point in my life. Together, with my lovely wife Ahlmira, we had the privilege of attending Randy Clark's School of Healing at Hosanna Lutheran Church in Lakeville, Minnesota. It was there we received a powerful impartation of the Father's Blessing that radically transformed our lives. We did not plan to attend the event; instead we came to participate in a mission consultation a week earlier. However, God had a different idea. He made a way for us to be where He wanted us to be.

During one of the sessions at the conference, Leif Hetland preached a powerful message that God used to spark something within us. The message was about the Father's love and Healing the Orphan Spirit. Leif shared his testimony of his encounter with the revelation of the Father's love and how it radically transformed his life. At one point he mentioned there are orphan ministries and orphan ministers who are out in the field trying to please God much like the older brother in the parable of the Prodigal Son. I felt in my spirit that I'd been an orphan minister myself. I then asked God to heal my heart and renew my mind. In that moment, I felt the love of the Father come upon me through His Baptism of Love. Finally, I came to a life-changing revelation that He is indeed a Father unto me and I am His beloved son through Jesus. I experienced so much freedom within. I suddenly realized the futility of my strivings of trying to work for God for the inheritance that He has freely made available to me through Jesus.

> "This is my beloved son in whom I am well-pleased." Those words resonated to the core of my being, rearranging and uprooting things within which had been brought about by an orphan mindset. It was such a powerful moment, to step into a revelation that God indeed is our Father who loves us unconditionally and completely.

Leif released the Father's blessing to everyone much like the declaration of the Father to His beloved son, Jesus "This is my beloved son in whom I am well-pleased." Those words resonated to the core of my being, rearranging and uprooting things within which had been brought about by an orphan mind-set. It was such a powerful moment, to step into a revelation that God indeed is our Father who loves us unconditionally and completely. What's more, we asked Leif to be our spiritual father. By God's favor, he accepted us into his spiritual family. This was a tremendous blessing for us. We felt we finally came out of the orphanage that very moment and received immeasurable inheritance from our spiritual father.

After that, we went back to the Philippines radically transformed. From that moment, we saw fruit coming forth—tremendous blessings, anointing and favor flowing to us and through us, such that we had never experienced in our lives before that moment.

Since that encounter in May 2006, God has literally poured upon us countless blessings through all aspects of our lives: family, finances, influence, health, anointing, and ministry. We have experienced the tangible fruits of favor. The doors of opportunity swung wide open, and the needed resources followed. Since receiving our Baptism of Love, from beginning with just one nation, Malaysia, we've now opened church planting works in Singapore, Cambodia, Vietnam, and Dubai. We have had opportunities to minister in other nations like Tanzania, India, and Pakistan through the ministry of Leif Hetland and Global Mission Awareness, as well as through our partnership with Hosanna Lutheran Church. We have seen major expansion in our movement, especially in the area of church planting locally and internationally. We've seen God move powerfully in our midst with mighty signs, wonders, and healings. Along with major breakthroughs in our ministry, we have been experiencing tremendous material blessings. The supernatural has become so natural to us.

We have released an impartation to our spiritual sons

and daughters, as well as the rest of our Destiny family. We have witnessed the increase of favor and blessings in the lives of our people. There has been so much abundance, holistically, in the lives of our people. In businesses, families, relationships, and ministries we have seen God's goodness flow from one person to another. Many have come to know the Lord because of the goodness they have experienced in their lives as the Destiny people have gone out releasing and praying blessings over multitudes of people. The blessings have come in health, radical healings, supernatural provision, employment, increases in income, restoration of relationships, and much more.

To me the greatest blessing I received was in May 2006. It was the revelation and the genuine encounter of Father's love that has continuously and progressively embraced me. Finally, I was out of the orphanage. I am now in my Father's house. I have been brought back to Eden, the place of His delight and affection. Father's unconditional and perfect love to me was the very power that brought me deeper and deeper into His presence. I was so hungry for His love, His voice, and His face. I know He will be there every time I set my heart and my affection towards Him. I feel so much freedom. Greater measures of His glory come to me each time I am with my Father.

Prior to this encounter of Father's love, I tried my best to wait upon the Lord in silence for at least an hour. Many times I did it out of discipline and striving. I had experienced levels of breakthroughs in my personal life and ministry, but it was hard living up to those breakthroughs while trying to please God with a mindset of an orphan. However, with the revelation of Father's love and that in Christ I am now completely loved and accepted, my motivation shifted from striving to perform, to delighting in Him because I know He delights in me. I am a prisoner in the arms of my Father God who loves me as He loves Jesus, His beloved son. I so love it! There are no more walls, no more condemnation, and no more striving. There's only love, only delight, and only goodness.

We are Entitled to the Same Baptism of Love

God sent Jesus so a Father and Son could demonstrate what love looks like. Two thousand years ago Father God looked upon Jesus as He was standing in the Jordan River, and the world became a blur. It was as if no one else was there, for His eyes focused on Jesus alone. His opening line spoke volumes of what He felt when He said, "This is my Son…" So no one would misinterpret the depth of the relationship between Father and His Son, He clarified it by saying, "I love my Son." For good measure the Father added, *"I am well-pleased with my Son."*

The world cannot fathom the love of our Father for His Son. We are more astounded by His sacrifice, for the Father loved the world so much that He gave the most precious thing He possessed—His one and only child. The Apostle Paul was one hundred percent correct when he said that for *our* benefit the Father did not spare His own Son. Would our loving Father then withhold the *Baptism of Love* from you and me? I believe Daddy God is longing to pour out His love on you and me.

Chapter Four

The Revelation of Security in Father God's Embrace

There are so many things I do not know. I don't claim to be an expert on everything, but there is one thing I am sure of—and that is—every man, woman, and child needs to feel secure. This is because insecurity is a destructive and unsettling feeling. Bill Johnson puts it this way, *"Insecurity is wrong security exposed."* Insecurity is both a driving force and a source of dread. Quite simply, insecurity is a symptom of an orphan spirit. People are driven to perform while others are afraid to enter into relationships for fear of ridicule and betrayal. While we understand the phenomenon called insecurity, it is important to know that Jesus never had to struggle with this negative feeling. He was the most secure person who ever walked this planet. He knew who He was and whose He was. Now, here's the good news, what is true for Him can also be true for you.

Jesus always felt secure. This stems from an ironclad assurance of Him knowing He was the Son of God. This revelation was like a cocoon, which covered Him from head to toe when the Spirit of His Father came down upon Him. His ears heard the declaration of the Father, while, at the same time, His inner being received the affirmation that He, indeed, was the one and only Son of God. The Father whispered in His ear and left a mark that could not be erased by anyone. This is the only thing He needed to know so He could be strong, stable, and secure. Jesus never had to contend with any form of identity crisis, and He never had to second-guess His true value in the eyes of His Father. However, the same cannot be said for everyone, especially not for those who have yet to encounter Father's love.

A World Afflicted with Father-Hunger

I had the privilege of speaking in a conference sponsored by the American Psychiatrist Association. My dear friend, Steve Mory, invited me to speak to this group. They were an amazing group because they were highly educated and yet they believed in God. One of the things I spoke to them about was what I believe to be the main root cause of all the social ills in America…*father-hunger.* That caught their attention.

I knew they were familiar with the concept of *father-hunger*, but they probably had put another label on it. We all had an understand-

> *The effect of father-hunger is well-known: insecurity, low self-esteem, violence, paranoia, anger, bitterness, self-hatred, suicidal thoughts, promiscuity, rebellion, confusion, restlessness, depression, addictions, compulsive behavior, despair, mental problems, etc. Yet, health professionals are seldom aware of the existence of an effective cure that can wipe away all the sadness and pain.*

ing that a father's embrace, a father's nurture, and a father's guidance, are sorely lacking in the world. From a scientific point of view, psychiatrists are intimately knowledgeable about this problem, but, unfortunately, many don't understand the cure.

The effect of *father-hunger* is well-known: insecurity, low self-esteem, violence, paranoia, anger, bitterness, self-hatred, suicidal thoughts, promiscuity, rebellion, confusion, restlessness, depression, addictions, compulsive behavior, despair, mental problems, etc. Yet, health professionals are seldom aware of the existence of an effective cure that can wipe away all the sadness and pain.

A long list of problems without a solution is not a good thing for mankind. Thank God this is not the truth. The Word of God is not ignorant of these issues, and it offers a cure: Jesus Christ. He is the way, the truth, and the life. He is the way to the Father. He revealed His Father to a broken and lost world. He has given us new life that we may have the right and the privilege to share in the love of Daddy God. We can also enjoy that love for all eternity and not go through a lifetime filled with insecurity.

Quite a number of the psychiatrists in attendance were professors in some of the top universities in America. I told them it does not matter who we are, what profession we are in, or the accomplishments we have achieved, if there is a person underneath our fancy exteriors, there is a person who feels like a failure. This is due to: no matter how hard we try to be the best we can be, we still feel we are a failure and we can never measure up.

There is a law out there we may not be aware of, and we are being judged according to its statues and precepts. There are spiritual laws of greater significance than the Constitution and other man-made ordinances. We know that if we are under the Law and examined according to its standards, we will surely fail the test.

All of us had an "F" on our report cards. However, there is hope for you and me because Jesus traded the "A" on His report card for our "F". He wants you to take His report card, and hand yours over to Him. He wants an exchange of life: His perfect and abundant life, for your problem-prone existence.

When I told that group of psychiatrists about this great exchange, there were several in the audience who began to weep. Many of them left that conference with the knowledge that there is a better way to deal with their hopeless cases, and that it is to pinpoint *father-hunger* and administer the love of Father God.

We need to learn how to enter into the Presence of our Father and experience the same affection. It is part of our rights and our privilege as children of God. Father even dares us to taste and see by saying, *"Draw near to me and I will draw near to you.."* (see James 4:8) We simply must make the first step, making our intentions known to Him, because our Father in heaven will never violate our will. He has given us a free will to choose because true love and coercion cannot co-exist (see 1 Corinthians 13:5).

It requires complete surrender, and we need to learn to take off our masks and present our true self, all of our blemishes and all our hurts, before a loving God. When we surrender, Father God will then take all those insecurities and fears and replace them with the love of a true Father.

Our Christian walk with our Father is a two-way street, a give and take. It requires complete surrender, and we need to learn to take off our masks and present our true self, all of our blemishes and all our hurts, before a loving God. When we surrender, Father God will then take all those insecurities and fears and replace them with the love of a true Father.

Jesus Rests in the Security of His Father's Embrace

Before Jesus launched into the deep, before He started his ministry, His Father took Him aside and spoke words to this effect, *"You are my Son; I love you; I am so happy I am your Father, and I am so proud of you."* It was a tremendous thing for a Dad to say to His Son. What do you think was the impact of those words? Try to imagine your own earthly

65

father taking time to be with you and talk to you heart-to-heart, candidly revealing what is inside his heart and mind and then giving the assurance that you are loved. I believe you would be in seventh heaven. But, more than that, you would have a wonderful sense of security.

The Father's declaration over the Son was a deep foundation that resulted in the creation of an impregnable fortress guarding His heart and mind from the attacks of the enemy. Humans are prone to bondage and require deliverance from something as mundane as bad habits, to something as serious as demonic oppression, because we do not have the capability to stand firm against the devil and the world. But Jesus didn't need to struggle due to the impressive defense His Father built in Him. His Father's embrace and words of affection secured Jesus from the evil onslaught of wickedness.

Let me clarify by giving an illustration. The American school system is befuddled by a problem called school bullying. This is an interesting and, at the same time, disturbing phenomenon because of the psychological and emotional impact bullying can have on a child. What really intrigues me is the capability of one child or a group of juveniles to terrorize an entire campus, and the subsequent inability of the student body and school officials to deal with the problem and end bullying for good.

What is even more unique is the fact that bullies come in different shapes and sizes. A bully does not need an imposing physique to become a child's worst nightmare. He simply needs to say the right words and learn to choose his victims. The effect is simply pitiful: children peeing in their pants, school age boys and girls faking sickness because they dread the thought of going to class, and children developing low self-esteem; often times incurring a profound psychological and emotional wounding that can take years to heal.

Again, I claim no expertise in this field, but I would like to suggest something. I would love to see fathers take time off from their busy schedule and talk to their sons and daughters in the most sincere and loving manner. They must speak out the words their children are longing to hear, *"You are my child, I love you and I am so happy to be your Daddy. You can come to me anytime and talk to me about anything you need at home or in school, and I will make time for you."* The father must first "educate" his children at home before he can expect them to receive formal education in school. They must learn their real value and their identity as a member of a family.

What do you think is the impact of a father's tender words? They leave a feeling of deep and lasting security in the heart and mind of the child. The same thing can be seen in the Father-Son relationship of Jesus Christ and his Daddy God.

By the way, did you know Jesus had a confrontation with a bully? He sure did. After His *Baptism of Love,* Jesus had to kick-start his ministry with a forty-day fast. After seven straight weeks without food, Jesus was famished and weak from lack of nourishment. This was the time when the father of all bullies came into the picture. Satan said words to this effect, *"Jesus, I am not convinced you are the Son of God. But if you are really the Son of God, then prove it by transforming these stones into bread."* It was a bully-tactic, forcing someone to commit a mistake in order to humiliate that person.

Jesus was hungry to His very bones, and Satan presented a very tempting offer. But Jesus understood His "Sonship" and His identity was never based on "power" and material wealth. His power was just a small part of the Father-Son relationship. In fact, the more important aspect of "Sonship" was the way He could hear His Father's voice and cling to His every word for sustenance and guidance (see Matthew 4:4). In the case of Jesus, what were the words Father gave to Jesus? He told Him, *"You are my Son."* And it was enough to keep him going through forty days of fasting and to survive relentless counter-attacks from the enemy.

> **We have a natural instinct to long for a father's embrace.**

Our Security Lies in the Finished Work of Christ Jesus

One of the major root causes of all the social ills in this

country is *father-hunger*. We have a natural instinct to long for a father's embrace. It is the right of every child to receive love. Yet, many have been deprived of this basic right. Because of sin, many are either born orphans, are abandoned, neglected, abused, and forgotten, but we praise God our Father who gave us the assurance we are no longer slaves, nor rebels, but sons.

Leanne Goff, my Personal Assistant and a spiritual daughter, shares her story of her *Baptism of Love*:

I came to Christ September 1976. I wanted to tell anyone and everyone about my newfound lover, Jesus. In less than five years, my husband, who came to Christ eight months before me, and I were on our first mission trip to Honduras. Our hearts were immediately captured with a desire to bring the Good News we had received to the nations.

Two years later, with our two young children, we went to Youth With A Mission (YWAM) for training. Over several years we were either living in Mexico, nations in Central America, or living stateside hosting teams to these nations. In 1992, we were invited to work with Teen Challenge in Iowa as Evangelism Supervisors. We served with Teen Challenge just short of ten years. I eventually became the Women's Director for Teen Challenge in Chattanooga, TN.

In June 2002, we were offered the opportunity to move back to Mexico and work with another ministry. We resigned our positions with Teen Challenge and headed south.

Things did not go as we thought in Mexico, and our stint was short lived. After five months, we moved back to the states—to Iowa. I was devastated. I did not want to be in back in the states, much less Iowa. I spiralled down into a state of depression, eventually on anti-depressants, something I never would have envisioned. I was a wreck and nobody knew what to do with me. I lived this way for months, giving up on anything and everything.

Because of my striving orphan mentality to prove myself and be accepted, I felt we had failed and God would never use us again on the mission field.

Prior to our move to Mexico, my son-in-law would tell me about a revival in Toronto, Canada. I had been to the Brownsville Revival many times, but had no desire to go to Toronto. But one day after our move to Iowa, I threw myself on our living room floor and cried out to God. I told Him, "Something has to change in my life. I know you did not create me to live this way. I don't care anymore about my reputation, my ministry, my credentials, titles, or who knows me or doesn't know me. I lay them all down before you." Something began to shift in that moment.

*I soon found out that our church was taking their first team to the revival in Toronto (known as The Father's Blessing). I was one of the first to sign up. I was a desperate woman. Prior to the trip, I remember telling my pastor, "I know Jesus as not only my savior, but my friend. I am very close to Him. But I still have a hard time with God as my Father. I know He is Father, but **my Father**?" I know this had a lot to do with my biological father being totally detached from me through my entire life. He never wanted to have anything to do with me, though he was obviously a significant part of my being created. I had the same image of Father God. He created me, but didn't want to have anything to do with me. He tolerated me, but didn't celebrate me. Many times, if I needed something or wanted something from Father God, I would ask my brother, Jesus, to ask Him because I knew He'd do it for Him. In my mind, this was the ultimate of an orphan mind-set.*

As soon as I walked into the church in Toronto, I sensed a love that I had NEVER sensed before. I was desperate, but so expectant! The first service began and our team was seated in the very back of this huge room of approximately four thousand people from all over the world. At one point during worship, John Arnott asked for the large group from Mexico to raise their hands. To my delight, this group was seated very close to us. John then asked the entire group to come forward. Then I heard John say, "Anyone who speaks Spanish....". Well that's all I needed.

I went forward to be prayed for, as well. God had set me up! See, I thought they were going to pray for those that spoke Spanish, too. How silly, huh? But what John said was, "Anyone who speaks Spanish, would you come up and help us pray for these brothers and sisters from Mexico?"

So I found myself up front with all these dark skinned, black hair Hispanics, with my eyes closed and in position to be prayed for. It's been said by what happened next, that in my desperation, I stole the birthright. Someone, a nobody, on their ministry team came along and just barely touched me and prayed, "More Lord". Well that was it! I landed on the floor and began to wail. I cried and cried for two and one-half hours. During this entire time, I felt the love of my Father, like I had never felt before, flow in and through my being, over and over again. I was stuck to the floor not being able to move. I was caught up into a love experience with my Father God that literally transformed my life.

*When I got up off the floor, my life had been drastically impacted. I had been baptized in His **perfect love**. It wasn't a touch, or a change; it was a transformation that has radically altered my life and ministry since. Many family and friends who have known me through the years are a witness to this transformation.*

At that point, God became my Dad. He's the best Dad

in the whole world, and I know that I can go to Him at anytime with anything. He has told me, "Leanne, you've been a Woman of God, a woman of integrity, and a successful minister with a heart after Me.

When I got up off the floor, my life had been drastically impacted. I had been baptized in His perfect love. It wasn't a touch, or a change; it was a transformation that has radically altered my life and ministry since.

But I don't want a Woman of God anymore. My desire is to have a little girl who knows she has a big Daddy". So now, that's my identity—A little girl with a BIG Daddy who loves me, is pleased with me, delights in me and finds me extraordinarily valuable! I'm no longer fatherless!

As our Father descends on us and wraps His loving arms around us, the father-hunger that used to be embedded deep within our hearts will be replaced by a spirit of Sonship; and we learn how to cry, *"Abba Father."* This is more than a happy encounter with God. More importantly, we have access to Him twenty-four hours a day, seven days a week, the whole year round and for the rest of eternity. We have the full rights as a son and a daughter of the Almighty God. If you are hidden in Christ, you will never be alone!

Our Father's embrace is not just a temporary feeling of joy, but an abiding presence. The moment Father baptizes you in His love you become an object of affection. This is not a new thing. Thousands of years ago God revealed the extent of His commitment to a group of men and women, former slaves who used to labor in Egypt. Through Moses we are told of God's compassion and intense desire to be with them, to nurture and to protect:

> *"He found him in a desert land, And in the wasteland, a howling wilderness; He encircled him, He instructed him, He kept him as the apple of His eye.*
>
> *As an eagle stirs up its nest, Hovers over its young, Spreading out its wings, taking them up, carrying them on its wings..."*
>
> Deuteronomy 32:10-11

In this passage of scripture, God reveals to us how he took care of His chosen people. He was like a dedicated tracker who kept searching, and when He found what He was looking for, He became a sentinel. He encircled the one He loved and zealously protected him like the apple of His eye. God was also depicted, as a mother eagle hovering over its young, and, if needed, would never hesitate to spread His wings to fly His beloved out of harms way. If this kind of commitment and passion was made available to people who were under the Law, how much more will He lavish love on you – a person whom He purchased with the life of His own Son?

Relying on Man-Made Security

People amass securities thinking they can be used as a hedge against emergencies and other problems. But as the stock market has been unstable in the past, we know we cannot rely on this type of security.

It is easy to be duped into buying something that promises to assuage our fears. These are safety nets padded with money, or they may be the creation of a network of so-called friends who can be relied on in times of need. I'm not saying we should become financially irresponsible and not think about the future. What I am saying is problems will come, like night follows day. Trials and tribulations are part of life, and there are many things we cannot predict. We cannot put our trust in man-made institutions. General Motors, Lehman Brothers, and Enron are just some of the companies that used to be considered as sure winners. In their advertisements, they promised us that once you got in, everything was going to be fine. However, it did not turn out that way! There were massive layoffs, and many people lost everything they owned, including money saved for retirement.

There must be another way. Our security must be founded on something more secure. Jesus proved to us He is the way, the truth, and the life when He laid down His life, and on the third day He rose from the grave. He had absolute control over life and death (see John 10:18). No one in human history was able to accomplish that feat. Death is always the equalizer, the single event feared by all. So what can you say to the one who destroyed death once and for all? He is the one you should have on your side every single day.

Jesus also said He is not a mere "hired hand" paid to watch over the flock. He declared He is the true Shepherd who will not hesitate to lay down His life for one single sheep. This is real security, friends. There is nothing like it in the whole wide world. Trust in the Lord. As Jesus was secure in His Father's embrace, you also will remain in that divine security knowing that He is committed to you.

> *Father's embrace is yours because whatever is true for Jesus has been made true for you.*

The night before His crucifixion, Jesus took bread, gave thanks, broke it, and gave it to His disciples with one solemn request, *"This is my body given to you; do this in remembrance of me."* (Luke 22:19, NIV) All we need to do is to simply remember Jesus and what He promised and what He has done for us, and then everything is made available to us. There is no need to endure the pain of abandonment, loneliness, and insecurity. Father's embrace is yours because whatever is true for Jesus has been made true for you.

Chapter Five

The Revelation of Father God's Approval

Christianity is different from other world religions. The others are all based on what man can do for God, while Christianity is all about God reaching out and doing everything needed to save man from sin and condemnation. The followers of false religions are forced to carry a load too heavy just so they can be proven worthy of the crumbs that fall from their master's table. But our Father in heaven has already demonstrated His unconditional love for you and

> *The carnal mind cannot comprehend affirmation without accomplishment, but we do not need to prove ourselves if we know we are already approved.*

me when He made a way to reconcile man to God while we were still rebels and sinners. It was a world-changing revelation.

Two thousand years ago another radical statement was made when Father God descended on the Jordan River to introduce His Son to the world. Even though Jesus had no track record to speak of, the Father said He was well pleased with His son. The carnal mind cannot comprehend affirmation without accomplishment, but we do not need to prove ourselves if we know we are already approved.

If a person has not yet experienced Father's *Baptism of Love*, then he or she is always under pressure to perform, to excel, and to succeed. We do this in order to earn God's approval. It is an acquired trait after a lifetime of receiving pain instead of love. We carry the emotional scars that came via words spoken by our earthly fathers. Many times a child will do his best to please his father, but, instead of affirmation, he receives criticism. This is a phenomenon we can call *"father-wounding"*.

We talked about *father-hunger* in the previous chapters. This is distinguished by the actions of an absentee father or an emotionally detached dad who has no time for his children and family. Father-wounding, on the other hand, is the withholding of approval. In this section, we will see that children are not only in need of their father's embrace and emotional nurture, but they also long for their father's approval.

Approval Must not be Given on the Basis of Merit, but Love

My dog will bark, jump, roll on the floor, and follow me around just to receive a furious rubbing of his fur. It is often times noisy and messy when this pet of mine tries to get my attention. His relentlessness is due to the constant need for my approval. If an animal longs for approval, how much more do people, especially children who look up to their fathers? Yet often, instead of the thumbs-up sign, we receive a thumbs-down gesture, reducing our perceived value even lower.

There may have been times when you gave your report card to your father. Your grades were good and you expected some form of congratulatory remark for all the hard work you had put into your studies. However, you did not receive anything of that sort—no embrace, no reward. Instead, your father told you that you could do better. It was a subtle way of rejecting you, although he may not have perceived it as such. It can be a typical reaction from a dad, won't you agree?

Many fathers do this without considering the impact of such an action. But, unbeknownst to many families and fathers all over the world, an emotional wound has developed deep within the spirit of their sons and daughters. The sting of the father-wounding can be a slow progressing poison, but effective, nonetheless, because it can change the whole personality and demeanor of a child. An infant is a happy bundle; he was born that way. Now, why is it that in a few years time, we can already sense a not-so-encouraging transformation?

As time passes, the child develops habits contrary to the innocence and carefree attitude of the person he was meant to be. A father looks into the face of his drug-addicted child and can no longer recognize him. *"This is not my first-born son,"* he says. A mother looks into the face of her sin-ravaged daughter and feels a rising panic, as she is unable to understand why a once precocious child is now staring inwardly into the dark emptiness of her mind. What has the child picked up along the way?

My dear friend, Jack Frost, who is now in heaven, tells his story in his book, *Spiritual Slavery to Spiritual Sonship* (used by permission from Shiloh Place Ministries):

> *Phileo is a Greek word meaning "demonstrated natural affection". (see John 16:27) It is used often in the Bible to describe God's love. Yet I always tended to view God's anointing as His power—or His supernatural ability to do great things. I had no idea that His anointing could actually be a demonstration of His unconditional affection for me. I was so locked into this trap of performance orientation that I still did not break free from my aggressive striving—even after a powerful visitation of God's Spirit! In fact, as I experienced more favor and notoriety in ministry, my addiction to striving grew even stronger!*

> *At that point my family had experienced enough of what I wrongly called "ministry." My wife and children knew I was worshipping a golden calf of self-centered religious pride. The ministry was all I talked about, all I lived for, and all that brought a smile to my face. I felt inadequate at expressing love and care for my family, so I gave myself to what I could do well—the ministry. It made everyone at home miserable. Trisha had had more than she could take. Our marriage was teetering on the*

edge of disaster.

Thinking that it was Trisha who had the real prob-lem, I took her to a conference on emotional healing in November 1995. I wanted her to be happy with how God was using me in ministry, so she would finally develop an appreciation for all the sacrifices I had made for her.

During an afternoon pastors' session, many of the wives were at the front receiving prayer. Trisha was resting on the floor, praying and weeping quietly as I knelt beside her. Then someone from the platform began to pray. The words startled me:

"Father God, take all the men in this room who were never held by their fathers. Hold them close right now. Give them the love their fathers did not know how to give."

The anointing of the Holy Spirit fell on me immedi-ately. I did not understand what was happening, but I knew something significant had begun to happen in my soul. I began crying like a baby as I lay at the altar. Such displays of emotion were not normal for me. I always had every emotion in check, especially in front of my wife, children, or other ministers. But my mask was off now. I was completely undone.

It was as if God transported me back to a time when

I was only ten. I suddenly saw vivid scenes of me as a child, hiding in a closet at night, fearful of the yelling and screaming I heard in my parents' room. I remembered the fear, the loneliness, and the sense of abandonment. I felt the deep, painful ache for my father's embrace—an embrace he was not able to give me during my childhood.

Suddenly I realized that now, thirty-four years later, my heavenly Father was meeting the deepest need in my heart for a natural demonstration of a father's affectionate love. I had a direct encounter with the phileo of God. As I lay on the floor weeping, Father God entered that dark closet of my childhood and held me in His arms. For forty-five minutes it was as if warm, liquid love flowed through my body and washed away much of the guilt, shame, fear of failure and rejection, fear of intimacy, and the fear of receiving and giving love.

My breakthrough finally came. My pride had been shattered. Until that moment I had never realized how deeply in bondage I was to striving and fear. But in that instant I felt free, and for the first time I experienced true rest. I had heard all my life that God loved me, but I had never lowered the walls of protection enough to personally receive a natural demonstration of His love and affection. Knowledge of His love had become a personal experience! Phileo was no longer just a Greek word to use to construct a theology.

I didn't stop weeping for five months. Every time I looked into my wife's eyes, or saw the pain that I had caused my children because of my lack of tenderness, the tears would begin to flow. Then I would kneel at their feet, weeping

The Father's affectionate phileo love began to restore the heart of this father to his children, and the hearts of my children to their father, and it was breaking a curse off of our lives.

and pleading for forgiveness for the times I had harshly misrepresented the Father's love to them.

I knew the healing would not come instantly for them. My children's hearts had been closed to me for years. But now, the brokenness I was experiencing began to open their spirits. The Father's affectionate phileo love began to restore the heart of this father to his children, and the hearts of my children to their father, and it was breaking a curse off of our lives (see Malachi 4:6).

This overpowering revelation of the Father's love also began transforming my marriage, but it didn't happen overnight.

I had rarely been able to pray with or minister to my wife prior to my encounter in 1995. In spite of the break-throughs I experienced with my children, something in me seemed to hold back from pursuing deeper levels of inti-

macy with Trisha. Because of some traumatic experiences of my childhood, I always kept my emotions and feelings under control around her. I daily said the words, "I love you," but I could not let Trisha inside. I did not want to risk being hurt again.

In March 1996 I went with a group of men to a conference in Canada, seeking a deeper revelation of God's love. During the first meeting, a lady at the altar prayed with me about some deep hurts I had encountered as a young boy. Through the supernatural leading of the Holy Spirit, this woman discerned that around age ten I had constructed thick walls of protection in my soul during the time that my father and mother were having extreme difficulties in their marriage.

This woman's prayers laid my heart bare. I lay on the floor weeping uncontrollably for two hours as the Father poured His comfort, love and affection into my wounded heart. When I got up, I knew that the wounds I experienced so long ago had been healed.

Then, during a subsequent ministry time that evening, what seemed like a river of God's love broke through all my fears of intimacy, and the walls I built so long ago began to crumble. For the next four days I wept as I realized the depth of pain Trisha lived with daily. She had always been kept at arm's length from the heart of her husband. I had unconsciously pushed her away. But when I arrived home from that conference I intimately ministered my love to her in healing prayer. She wept for hours as the Father took her back to some points of deep wounding in her youth, comforting her with His healing love.

God began to take our relationship into new depths of intimacy. We have hit a few stumbling blocks along the way, but each time the Holy Spirit would reveal past hurts where we had built walls of protection. We would move toward repentance, and the love of God would wash away hidden barriers and take us into deeper depths of love for each other.

We were created to grow from glory to glory; but, with father wounding, we are forced to create a wall of defense, develop a lying tongue,

> The cycle may go on and on, if not for the cure— the life-transforming love of our Father God.

isolate ourselves, and pretend to be happy. At a young age, many learn how to cope with the effects of father wounding. After a few years, the relationship between father and son grows cold and distant. This is because the son or the daughter cannot risk another "episode" with their daddy. If only the father would have been aware that the child was diligently seeking his approval, then I believe he might have been more gracious. Understandingly, he may have also received the same *father-wound* from his father, being passed down from grandfather, to father, to son. The cycle may go on and on, if not for the cure—the life-transforming love of our Father God.

Counterfeit Affections vs. the Balm of Gilead

Affirmation from our parents, our spouse, and our friends, are oftentimes hard to come by. We receive few commendations, and we give out few because we base our praise on a merit system when it should be rooted in love. This is why many people spend their lives trying to earn love when all they need to do is receive love.

It comes to a point when the need for approval becomes desperate while, at the same time, the wounds we receive from the people we love become too painful. Consequently, we are driven to seek comfort through counterfeit affections. A counterfeit is a lie masquerading as truth—an imitation of what is real and valuable. It is a path that is wide and smooth, but leads to desolation.

There are many forms of counterfeit affections present in the world. Sexual immorality may look and feel like real love shared by a man and a woman. However, at the end, there is so much suffering and pain. Recreational drugs may feel so good, imitating the feeling of real joy. They produce rapturous ecstasy at the beginning, but eventually, the body is destroyed along with the soul. It may seem like the real thing, yet it is counterfeit. As the very wise King Solomon said, *"There is a way that seems right to a man, but in the end it leads to death.* " (Proverbs 14:12, NIV) Interestingly, we know that counterfeit affections bring spiritual death. But most times our love deficits are too much to handle, so we embrace it to soothe our pain because, at the point of despair, death is seen as a welcome respite.

There are Christians who understand perfectly well that counterfeit actions are the devil's tools to lead us astray. They are also familiar with the Balm of Gilead—a very effective healing ointment—one of the names used to describe Jesus. He alone can heal the most hard to reach places of a sick and broken heart. Yet, many Christians do not know how to obtain and apply the Balm of Gilead. They think they have to work for it. They assume they have to perform in order to earn it, when they actually only need to be in a position to receive.

The Inherent Value of a Child

Let's say that you are sick with an incurable disease: a sickness that not only weakens you but is also a source of torment. You have tried everything to ease the pain, and yet death stares you in the face. Then one day someone approaches you and says there is a cure. He shows you a picture of the Balm of Gilead. From the looks of it, you can tell right away that it is an expensive ointment, encased in an elaborately designed jar. Your first reaction is to worry about the price, the difficulty of acquiring such treasure, and the effort needed to contact the seller. After reflecting on your current situation, you grab hold of the messenger's hands and begging him you say, *"I will do everything and give everything; just tell me where I can find this wondrous cure."* The messenger is puzzled with your question, and he replies, *"Your Father has an inexhaustible supply."*

Believe it or not, many Christians, who are caught in the crossroads of spiritual identity, question, *"Am I a slave or a child of God?"* Sometimes we are given a problem to force us into a decision. Moses was placed in the middle of a moral and spiritual dilemma in order to force him into a decision, *"Was he an Egyptian or an Israelite?"* One day he saw a taskmaster maltreating his fellowmen, and, instead of simply rebuking the Egyptian slave-driver, he murdered him and hid him because he did not want Pharaoh to find out he had sided with the slaves. He wanted to be Hebrew, connected to Yahweh. However, at the same time, he wanted to be an Egyptian prince. He could not have both. Moses had to choose.

Pharaoh found out about the conspiracy, and Moses fled for his life. He traveled far and resided in obscurity. Stripped of royal rank and humiliated, Moses tried to survive using his skills and wit, but for forty years he was unable to become the man he was destined to be. Then the LORD showed up and confronted Moses.

Moses had an encounter with God, and the LORD told him he was not just a caretaker of his father-in-law's sheep.

God revealed to Moses that he was more valuable than Egyptian royalty and that he was a Prince of God—a ruler of His people. However, Moses could not accept this gift. He could not receive healing, restoration, or promotion. He struggled and he rebelled against the appointment of God. Contrary to popular belief, there was no breakthrough for Moses on the mountaintop. The LORD had to pursue Moses when he went down from Mt. Horeb and into the wilderness because Moses refused to believe.

The Lord made His case, and Moses made his counter-argument. The debate went back and forth. Moses' fear and disobedience grew with each passing day. The LORD had to make another unnecessary appearance, and Moses had a re-encounter with God. Moses only began to have a change of heart when God declared, *This is what the LORD says, 'Israel is my firstborn son.'"* (Exodus 4:22) Moses' world was turned-upside-down when he received the revelation that God was their Father. The heart of the Father was revealed to him.

When Moses met the Israelites for the first time, he persuaded them to leave their place of torment, not because Yahweh was much better than the Nile goddess, but because He was a Father in love with His children.

The persistence of God and His love for the Israelites slowly transformed Moses' thinking. He understood that

God's attempt to meet and lead His people in this daring rescue was not about religion or self-glorification; it was all about love and a Father's concern for His long lost children. When Moses met the Israelites for the first time, he persuaded them to leave their place of torment, not because Yahweh was much better than the Nile goddess, but because He was a Father in love with His children. In Exodus 4:31, the Bible recorded their response to Moses' preaching, *"And when they heard the LORD was concerned about them and had seen their misery, they bowed down and worshiped."* As long as Israel remained under the spirit of Sonship, they were victorious; but the moment they reverted to a slave mentality, they were doomed.

Do You Have Any Idea That You Have a God-Appraised Value?

Moses was a failure in the eyes of the world. The most powerful citizens of the ancient world viewed him as a disgrace, a murderer, an impostor, and a social climber. In exile he was barely making a living by being a mere caretaker of livestock—for he could not even afford to have his own sheep, but the Father approved of him and gave him a high rating when Moses had nothing to prove his worth. Even when Moses turned his back on God, the Father was still relentless, being willing to climb the highest mountain and walk the driest valley just to convey a message of love. The Father showed everyone that He placed a premium on relationship when He said His name will forever be associated with His sons—Abraham, Isaac, and Jacob (see Luke 4).

The Hebrews were slaves when God approved them to be His people. In the eyes of Pharaoh, they were nothing and were appreciated only as mere earth-moving tools and beasts of burden, but the LORD saw something different. In His eyes, the scarred back, worn hands, and weak bodies were precious. He would glorify Himself through them, even if they were considered the weak things of the world, simply because they were His children. Father God used the strongest term of endearment understandable in the Eastern context when He said to Israel, *"You are my firstborn son."* If they received such love under the Law, how much more those who received forgiveness from sins through Jesus?

The children of Israel were God-approved because they received the right to be the children of God even when they had nothing with which to purchase it. During Jesus' *Baptism of Love*, He heard His Father say, *"I am well pleased with You."* This approval was given even before Jesus started healing the sick, casting out demons, raising the dead, feeding the multitudes, walking on water, binding storms, setting captives free, and teaching words of wisdom and grace. His Father made it clear that His approval was based on value, rather than performance.

Have you received your God-appraised value? If you haven't yet received this special blessing from your Father

God, then do not believe the appraisal of others, because they will surely undervalue you.

Do you know that a sparkling diamond, which is usually set on an expensive wedding ring, was originally found buried under a ton of debris or hidden in deep, murky waters? The average man or woman cannot tell an ordinary piece of stone from a diamond. A dazzling diamond is the by-product of a lengthy process under the hands of a master craftsman. This is the reason it is easy for others to ridicule a child of God. This diamond-in-the-rough identity problem is the same reason Christians do not value themselves and are unable to reach their full potential. They lack understanding in this regard.

Let's say you have a bit of knowledge about diamonds, and you find one covered with mud and dirt. Will you allow others to take it by force by deluding you into thinking it has no value because of its present condition? No way! I believe you will challenge their claim and fight for your right as the one who mined that expensive gemstone. Be aware, therefore, Father God will fight for His children (see John 17:9-12).

When Father looks at you, He knows your real value. Please don't go to religion or other forms of Christian legalism in order to find a fair appraiser, for there is a great chance what you will find are critics who will significantly reduce your self-worth. Before you know it, you will become like one of them. You will become like the religious Pharisees whose value is in the things they can do for God. However, your identity is not found in what you can do for God, but in what God has done for you. If your abilities, possessions, and the things you can do for God define you, then you will eventually use the same standard to judge other people.

The Bible says Jesus was without sin: He was blameless, but not because He worked at it like a Pharisee would. He saw things differently. We approach the Law of God from the vantage point of a slave; Jesus approached it from the perspective of a Son. Jesus was without sin because He was never driven to perform in order to seek His Father's approval. He was so full of the Father's love that He need not compare Himself to others.

> *We can only remain childlike if we are assured of our place in our Father's heart. Therefore, take a step forward, receive His approval, and receive His Baptism of Love.*

He was approved of God, and, therefore, He need not condemn others to make Himself feel better. He was not overburdened with guilt, and His mind was not preoccupied with the unnecessary. This is the reason there was room in His life to receive all heaven has to offer. He learned how to abide because He remained as a Son with a childlike attitude. Let us learn to receive in like manner. We can only remain childlike if we are assured of our place in our Father's heart.

Therefore, take a step forward, receive His approval, and receive His *Baptism of Love.*

Chapter Six

The Revelation of Supernatural Favor

The *Baptism of Love* experienced by Jesus in the Jordan River was not just an emotional experience. When Father expressed His love and longing for His Son, a deep transformation occurred in the life of Christ. Before this event, He was a mere carpenter, the son of Joseph and Mary. After His baptism, Jesus was known as the Son of God. The title bestowed on Him was just the beginning. Everywhere He went, no one He met could deny there was something special about Him. Favor rested on Him, and, in just three and half years of ministry, He made a lasting impact that continues to resound even to this day. His ministry changed the world. If we, too, are to have a ministry that makes an impact upon the people around us, we need to know how to walk like Jesus. We need to exercise our God-given authority like He did. We need to learn to speak with power and to expect results.

There was an unmistakable air around Jesus. The Pharisees, the High Priest, and even Pilate were reluctant to touch Him. On the other hand, children loved His presence and sinners congregated around Him. He was able to accomplish something that would require kings and tyrants a multitude of lifetimes to equal. The supernatural favor of God rested upon Him.

> For at long last, someone had come to take the seat of authority vacated by Adam. The Son of God had come to bring order to chaos.

It all began with one powerful declaration. Father said, "This is my Son..." and the whole world took notice. Demons began to quake. Politicians and religious leaders were dismayed while the natural and spiritual realms began to hum contentedly. For at long last, someone had come to take the seat of authority vacated by Adam. The Son of God had come to bring order to chaos.

The Father said, *"You are my Son..."* and the floodgates of heaven were opened, and spiritual gifts, revelation, and power were poured out on Jesus. No bronze door could stop Him, no storm could overturn His boat, and no mob could intimidate Him. He was not hindered by lack, and death could never hold Him. The Father's favor rested on Him.

Jesus was free from the law and man's ordinances, but when He chose to show His strength, He was mightier than an army in full battle array. There was no one who could stand before Him. He picked, pulled, plucked, hooked, and took hold of everything He needed to fulfill the call of God upon His life—from figs to spiritual fire—He had access to everything. The things He required were made available and ready. It all started with the words, *"This is my Son, whom I love, with Him I am well pleased."* Every living and non-living thing had to agree. Jesus made His relationship with His Father the starting point. Because of this attitude, His life and ministry was a showcase of what supernatural favor is all about. Jesus understood the dynamics that exist in a father-son relationship. We must learn to do the same.

Jesus' identity as the Son and the commendation He received from the Father created a platform for Him to stand upon and complete the work abandoned by the first Adam. He demonstrated how to rule and reign using a scepter of justice and mercy. He administered loving-kindness over the things His Father had given Him. The Baptism of Love gave Jesus the confidence, security, authority, and favor that would allow Him to move into the spiritual and physical realms with ease. We must experience the same thing.

I recall the story of D.L. Moody when his supernatural encounter of God's love transformed his life and ministry:

Moody's hunger for a deeper spiritual experience was deepened by the preaching of Henry Moorhouse, the famous English boy preacher, who visited Moody's church in Chicago soon after Mr. Moody returned to America. For seven nights Moorehouse preached from the text, John 3:16, "For God so loved the world, that he gave his only begotten Son, that whosoever believeth in him should not perish, but have everlasting life." Every night he rose to a higher and higher plain of thought, beginning at Genesis and going through the Bible to Revelation, showing how much God loved the world. He pointed out how God loved the world so much that He sent patriarchs and prophets, and other holy men to plead with the people, and then He sent His only Son, and when they had killed Him, He sent the Holy Ghost. In closing the seventh sermon from the text, he said: "My friends, for a whole week I have been trying to tell you how much God loves you, but I cannot do it with this poor stammering tongue. If I could borrow Jacob's ladder and climb up into heaven and ask Gabriel, who stands in the presence of the Almighty, to tell me how much love the Father has for the world, all he could say would be, 'God so loved the world, that he gave his only begotten Son, that whosoever believeth in him should not perish, but have everlasting life.'" Moody's heart was melted within him as he listened to the young preacher describing the love of God for lost mankind. It gave him such a vision of the love of God as he had never seen before, and from that time forward Moody's preaching was of a more deeply spiritual character.

Moody continued to hunger for a deepening of his own spiritual life and experience. He had been greatly used of God, but felt that there were much greater things in store for him. This realization was deepened by conversations he had with two ladies who sat on the front pew in his church. He could see by the expression of their faces that they were praying. At the close of the service they would say to him, "We have been praying for you." "Why don't you pray for the people?" Mr. Moody would ask. "Because you need the power of the Spirit," was the reply. "I need the power! Why," said he, in relating the incident afterwards, "I thought I had power. There came a great hunger into my soul. I did not know what it was. I began to cry out as I never did before. I really felt that I did not want to live if I could not have this power for service."

"My heart was not in the work of begging," says he. "I could not appeal. I was crying all the time that God would fill me with His Spirit. Well, one day, in the city of New York—oh, what a day!—I cannot describe it, I seldom refer to it; it is almost too sacred an experience to name. Paul had an experience of which he never spoke for fourteen years. I can only say that God revealed Himself to me, and I had such an experience of His love that I had to ask Him to stay His hand. His soul was set on fire in such a way that his work would soon become a worldwide one. (Copied by Stephen Ross for WholesomeWords.org from Deeper Experiences of Famous Christians... by J. Gilchrist Lawson. Anderson, Ind.: Warner Press, 1911.)

Father had no problem giving Jesus everything He asked for. He was authorized, deputized, baptized, and He was given the keys to heaven and earth. Jesus succeeded because He knew His place—it was revealed to Him when He was baptized in the love of His Father.

Father wants us to share the same supernatural favor as Jesus, D.L. Moody, Charles Finney and so many others have.

> *The Father's favor rested on Jesus because He remained in the correct attitude throughout His earthly life. We must allow Jesus to teach us how to be in submission and to be always longing for our Father's embrace.*

But first we need to learn how to walk as true sons of our Father. The Father's favor rested on Jesus because He remained in the correct attitude throughout His earthly life. We must allow Jesus to teach us how to be in submission and to be always longing for our Father's embrace.

Jesus: The Perfect Prototype Son

Jesus was in perfect harmony with His Daddy God; He showed the way. Everything He did was for our benefit. It was to model the right way of living. It was not just the suffering He had to endure so we could obtain the forgiveness for our sins. Every action and every word He spoke was meant to teach us how to live life to the fullest (see John 10:10). If we cannot see His legacy from this perspective, then we will make erroneous assumptions. His life, His words, and His deeds are part of our heritage. What belongs to Christ belongs to us. If we fail to grasp it in this manner, then we will most probably squander our inheritance.

We should thank our Father because He sent His only Son to show us how to live. Point-by-point and precept-by-precept, He demonstrated how to lead a life that attracts favor. He did not allow us to grope in the dark or discover by trial and error. He showed the way. He prayed, He was baptized in the Jordan, He fasted, He meditated on Scriptures, and He declared that the Kingdom of God had come and the will of His Father must be established on earth as it is in heaven. The most important thing Jesus modeled for us is the mindset of a true spiritual son.

It is also essential to point out that it was Father and Son teamwork. It was not a one-way-street relationship wherein Jesus was the only one who worked hard to please His Father. On the contrary, it was a beautiful partnership marked by reciprocity and intimacy between Father and Son. Jesus was in constant communion with His Father. He could have chosen to pray in a secluded spot, in a place far from prying eyes, and the Father could have privately spoken the same words of tenderness and approval, but it would have been selfish. So the Father and Son made a public display of affection, and it was for our benefit.

> *Jesus wanted to make sure we could know the key that will unlock supernatural favor by having a sensitive consciousness to the Father-heart of God. He is attracted to those who display an attitude of submission, honor, and love towards the Father. It is only through Sonship we can receive.*

Jesus wanted to make sure we could know the key that will unlock supernatural favor by having a sensitive consciousness to the Father-heart of God. He is attracted to those who display an attitude of submission, honor, and love towards the Father. It is only through Sonship we can receive. This is because the transfer of authority, power, and blessing can only flow one way—from a father to a son.

Sonship is a Keen Awareness of What Comprises a Father-Son Relationship

I want to reiterate, when I speak of father-son, this is not gender specific. Ladies, just as we men will be called the Bride of Christ throughout eternity, you too are sons of God. That said, a true son is sensitive to the inner working of a father-son relationship. He takes advantage of what is available to him. He is not ashamed to approach, ask, or receive. There is confidence rising up within him as he gets closer to his father because he knows he is the beloved of his dad. There is no double-mindedness: there is only a mind made up to adore and serve his father.

A rebellious son, on the other hand, does not care that he is unaware of the father's wishes. There is a profound level of ignorance and foolishness that exists within the rebellious spirit when it comes to his duties, obligations, and inheritance. Cain, Ham, and Esau exemplify this truth. They acted with contempt towards their birthright, their privileged position, and the unconditional love their fathers demonstrated toward them. However, when it comes to studying the implication of transgressing spiritual laws that govern a father-son relationship, there is perhaps no other story as haunting as that of Ham.

Ham was the son of Noah. A flood destroyed the only surviving patriarch in the whole world after the earth. Ham's family practically owned the entire planet. There was no one else who could contest his or her claim. God gave the whole earth to Noah to manage and occupy. In short, Ham was in a privileged position to ask and receive. The verse that says "Ask and I will give you the nations as your inheritance" (Psalm 2:8) was never a rhetorical statement for Ham. He could have asked for Asia or Europe, and he would have received it. Unfortunately, Ham squandered his inheritance and was left with nothing.

Ham was not even slightly aware of his status. He went into the ark with a pauper mentality, not a son or a prince, and came out of the ark with the same mindset. This led him to act like a fool and dishonor his father, Noah. What happened next is a chilling reminder not to take for granted the dynamics within a father-son relationship. Noah said, "Cursed be Canaan! The lowest of slaves will he be to his brothers." (Genesis 9:25) Take note that Noah cursed the son and not the father. Noah cursed Canaan, not Ham, because ultimately it is the son who will inherit the legacy of his father (see Psalm 2:7). Ham could have asked for the nations, but instead he reaped what he sowed. He bequeathed trouble instead of blessing to his offspring.

I hope you are seriously considering the implication of your Sonship made available through Jesus Christ. Father God is willing to unveil the benefits available to spiritual sons only if we are committed to walk the path prepared for those who believe. In order to have a keen awareness of the privileges and rights available to God's children, it is important to meditate on the *Parable of the Lost Son* and the Apostle Paul's letter to the Galatians. By doing so, we will come to understand that in the context of a father-son relationship; we can experience favor that comes from our Father. This is seen in the spirit of liberty that breaks the yoke of bondage and provides our access to the glorious riches in Christ Jesus, so we can finish the task given to us by our Father.

Freedom, according to Paul, is not the license to sin, but the capacity to become the person you were meant to be. You know the will of God for your life, but you are limited by fear and condemnation. It is for freedom that you've been set free (see Galatians 5:1). You were set free from the manipulations of men. No one can imprison you with threats of damnation and excommunication because you've been justified through faith in Christ. You've been set free from the bondage of sin. The old has gone; the new has come (see 2 Corinthians 5:17). This is why you can do more than ancient Israel. They were merely members of a chosen race, but we belong to the family of God. You are free to soar because you are no longer under a curse (see Galatians 3:10). You are free to complete the task because you have access to God's storehouse.

A keen sensitivity to what comprises a father-son relationship will help reveal the depth of supernatural favor available to us children. We have to arm our minds with this truth.

In *The Parable of the Lost Son*, the elder brother complained that he had worked long and hard, and yet the father did not give him a gift he could use to enjoy life and to sustain him for another day. The father's surprised reply was this, *"'My son,' the father said, 'you are always with me, and everything I have is yours.'"* (Luke 15:31) How many Christians suffer from burn out and their zeal for Father's Kingdom fades away? How many are unable to approach Papa God to receive the very thing they desperately need in order to succeed? *"Everything I have is yours"*, this is your Father speaking.

A keen sensitivity to what comprises a father-son relationship will help reveal the depth of supernatural favor available to us children. We have to arm our minds with this truth, *"You are all sons of God through faith in Christ Jesus, for all of you who were baptized into Christ have clothed yourselves with Christ."* (Galatians 3:26-27) When Father met Jesus in the Jordan River, He fitted Him with a robe of honor and wrapped Him with the cloak of power (see Luke 24:49). Our raiment is Christ. It is time to walk as true sons of our Father.

A Father's Authority and Influence Can Only Flow One Way: From Father to Son

The Apostle Paul did not make a mistake in his choice of words. He must have remembered two instances in scripture wherein fathers clothed their sons with a covering to symbolize the special bond that exists between parent and child. The first one is between a father and his biological son; the second one is between a spiritual father and his spiritual son.

The first instance happened between Jacob and Joseph. The second occurred between Elijah and Elisha. These two sons experienced favor from both God and man because their fathers made provisions for them to succeed. They were able to take hold of their dreams and shape history because their fathers initiated the transfer of power and blessing. Remember, it flows only one way—from father to son.

Joseph and Elisha behaved as true sons. We know that Jacob had other sons (eleven to be exact), but none of them acted in truth, honor, and love in the same way that Joseph behaved towards his dad. We also know that Elijah had numerous spiritual sons (at least fifty of them, according to the Bible), but none of them—except Elisha—stayed in perfect alignment. They were willing to observe from a distance; they were eager to learn but unwilling to walk side-by-side with their father and share in his sorrows, as well as in his victories.

Both Joseph and Elisha received double blessing and double anointing. In the life of Joseph, God illustrated the significance of maintaining an attitude of faithfulness, honor, and service. Joseph was never bitter toward his father or his brothers. As a result, something extraordinary had to be done to give him the blessing and honor he deserved.

When Jacob was about to die, he called Joseph and his two sons so he could bless them. Then Jacob did something amazing, he said to Joseph, *"Now then, your two sons born to you in Egypt before I came to you here will be reckoned as mine; Ephraim and Manasseh will be mine, just as Reuben and Simeon are mine."* (Genesis 48:5, NIV) Such a thing was never done before. In order to give a double portion to Joseph, his father, Jacob, had to bend what was natural and turn it into the supernatural. Jacob blessed Ephraim and Manasseh (his grandsons) as his own sons.

This explains why there are Benjaminites and there are Simeonites, but there are no "Josephites". Something had to be done in order for Joseph to receive more than just one portion. If this were not allowed to happen, then Jacob would have been forced to subdivide everything he owned and apportion his spiritual blessing—in a manner of speaking—equally among his twelve children. However, Joseph's actions called for more. So Jacob had to alter his family tree in order for Joseph to receive a double portion through his two sons.

When the nation of Israel entered the Promised Land, Ephraim and Manasseh were considered two separate tribes; therefore, they received an allotment just like the other sons of Jacob (see Joshua 17:17). This was arranged so Joseph's attitude and loyalty to his father would never go unnoticed for all of eternity, and would cause people to question and learn more about the actions of Joseph. People will question why there is a discrepancy whenever the Bible talks about the twelve tribes of Israel. If you count them, there are thirteen tribes, not twelve. Those who are spiritually aware will explain that God tremendously blesses those who walk with Him as a dutiful son walks with his father.

Perpetual Favor Rested on Jesus Christ

Joseph and Elisha received favor from on high because they were good sons. We, however, will receive favor not because we are inherently good, but because of what Christ has done for us. He not only showed the way, He also took the penalty for our sins. The consequence of our disobedience He took upon Himself. Thus, when we receive Jesus in our hearts through faith, we are hidden in Him.

> *When the Father sees us, He will grant the desires of our hearts because God can no longer see the old self, but He sees His Son in us. Christ is our raiment.*

When the Father sees

us, He will grant the desires of our hearts because God can no longer see the old self, but He sees His Son in us. Christ is our raiment. He is our robe of honor; He is our cloak of power. We receive this double blessing and double anointing by grace. We are adopted. The Father has altered His family tree. We, who were once aliens and slaves, have now become a part of His household. The moment we cease striving and maintain the correct attitude and imbibe the spirit of Sonship, we are able to cry "Daddy God". His ears will listen to our prayers, and He will descend on us. He comes in like a gentle whirlwind to overwhelm us with supernatural favor.

Chapter Seven

Experiencing the Baptism of Love

We have come to the end of our study. We have seen the tremendous blessing and favor that remained in and on Jesus after He received His baptism in the Jordan River. Love, favor, anointing, and power were in Jesus for Him, and on Him for us. It is the same with us…love, favor, anointing, and power are in us for us, and on us for others. If not for the sacrifice made on the cross, there would be no more discussion regarding this topic. If not for love, we are merely outsiders looking in. But thanks be to God our Father, we can dare raise this question, *"He who did not spare His own Son, but gave Him up for us all—how will He not also, along with Him, graciously give us all things?"* (Romans 8:32) Thankfully, we know the answer: the Father will never withhold any good thing from His children!

The triple baptism Jesus experienced in the Jordan River—the in filling of righteousness, power, and love – is also available to us. We only need to discover how to receive these gifts, especially the *Baptism of Love*, the least known among the three. It is important to remember that they all are to be received, and not achieved.

> *A review of Jesus' life and ministry will help reveal the secrets of Sonship and the correct mindset required to pull heaven towards earth.*

Once again, we thank

the Father for sending His one and only Son because He came as the firstborn among many so He could lead the way. A review of Jesus' life and ministry will help reveal the secrets of Sonship and the correct mindset required to pull heaven towards earth—to attract favor and to prepare a habitation so the dove will remain in us for us, and on us for others. We need the Spirit to be always in our midst, dwelling in the temple that is our body which is offered as a living sacrifice to God. Jesus modeled a life of victory and holiness. He demonstrated we could do the same if we possess godly knowledge, if we desire to pursue the Father-heart of God, and if we maintain the right attitude inherent in sons and daughters of Papa God.

If You Only Knew

When we become Christians—the tongue-talking, devil-chasing, Bible-believing kind—most of us begin to abandon our thirst for knowledge, wrongly thinking that theology is not good for the soul. We are told that excessive study puffs up the ego and inflates our self-image. We hastily conclude that it can ruin our relationship with God. However, the Bible is clear in this regard saying, *"The heart of the discerning acquires knowledge; the ears of the wise seek it out."* (Proverbs 18:15, NIV) In reading other translations, we can surmise that the heart of the prudent longs for knowledge; the wise man knows the eternal value of seeking after God's information.

There are many instances in the Bible where a person was limited, not by desire or integrity of heart, but by lack of knowledge. Take for instance Nicodemus. His heart was pure, but he could not receive more because he could not discern correctly. He was uninformed when it came

> *If we are unaware of the things that rightfully belong to us, then we will never ask for them. We will never ask the Father to bequeath blessings to us because the thought will never even cross our minds.*

to the more important things of God. When told about his need to be born again, Nicodemus was clearly confused and questioned, *"How can this be?"* (John 3:9, NIV) The Lord, however, had a quick reply saying, *"You are Israel's teacher … and do you not understand these things?"* (John 3:10, NIV) As a Christian, are there important spiritual truths of which we are not aware?

The lack of godly information can seriously affect our spiritual growth. If we are unaware of the things that rightfully belong to us, then we will never ask for them. We will never ask the Father to bequeath blessings to us because the thought will never even cross our minds. As a result, we can hear Father's lament, *"…my people are destroyed from lack of knowledge."* (Hosea 4:6, NIV)

I believe one of these heart-rending lessons was Jesus' encounter with a woman from Samaria. For the longest time, the Samaritan people had believed the lie that they were of no importance and that they had been barred entry into the holy mountain of God. They had no knowledge of their heritage as descendants of Abraham, and, therefore, heirs just like their neighbors the Israelites. Yet, Jesus had come to set the Samaritans free. His strategy was to transform the life of an adulterous woman, and He used her as God's mouthpiece to that region.

However, the Samaritan woman proved to be "a tough cookie", making all sorts of arguments as to why she was not worthy to receive. Nevertheless, Jesus needed only one statement to break down the walls of pride and sin. He said, *"If you knew the gift of God and who it is that asks you for a drink, you would have asked Him and He would have given you living water."* (John 4:10, NIV) Thus, Jesus "cut through to the chase". He indicated it was not her past, her sin, or her religious affiliation that hindered God from blessing her. It was her lack of revelation regarding her identity in Christ and what God had prepared for her. As with this Samaritan woman, if you only knew, then you would take action.

The Samaritan woman continued issuing excuses. She declared she was a five-time divorcee, that she was a victim of religious persecution, that she was a member of a minority, and that she was a woman with limited means. All of these issues were of no importance to Jesus, for He knew what was really wrong with her. She had no idea she was an heir to an ancient promise – the one Yahweh gave Abraham, Isaac, and Jacob.

She may have known she was descended from Israel (see John 4:12), but it was not enough to set her free. Jesus had to "turn on the lights" so she could see clearly. Jesus made her understand she was not only the descendant of the great patriarchs, but, more importantly, she was the daughter of God. Her breakthrough began when Jesus guided her to the truth. When her eyes were opened, she was able to receive the blessing of freedom from sin and the affirmation that she was beloved of God, regardless of sin, race or religion. This gift was already made available even before she was born, but she had been unaware of it. The Samaritan woman had to make a claim because she was entitled to it.

I would like to highlight what Jesus revealed to her. If I may have the liberty to interpret what the Lord said to the Samaritan woman, then I believe Jesus said something along these lines, *"If you are intimately aware of the gift of God, and if you only knew its real value and how it can make an impact to a lost and dying world, you would have asked Me, and then you would have promptly received. If you only knew the Father-heart of God, then you would have asked Him in My name, and He would have given you your heart's desire, because you know very well that He would not reject you, and He would not fail you."*

These words apply to us, as well. If we only understood the precious gift of God, we would ask Him. Sadly, many Christians are not in the position to receive because they have no idea how much their Father cares for them, and that He is eager to baptize them in His love. Nevertheless, knowledge and desire must come first before God will reveal Himself. This is because the Father will never violate our will. He waits for us to draw near.

David was After the Heart of Father God

We have heard the saying that zeal without knowledge is deadly, but knowledge without zeal is empty. Knowledge is not enough; it does not yield much. Knowledge must be coupled with desire, so that we will act on what we know. Because it does not totally matter what we know, our life's worth is measured by knowledge application, *not* knowledge acquisition. King Solomon was far more knowledgeable than King David, but he tore the kingdom in two. David ushered in the Golden Age of Israel, while Solomon was instrumental in its decline.

The major difference between these two kings was the level of their desire towards God. Solomon was more interested in the practical aspects of his reign. Such as, how to further his political goals, how to generate wealth, and how to keep his people happy. Solomon wanted to know more about the laws of God in order to become an effective leader. David, on the other hand, was interested in knowing more about the lawgiver and the King of kings. He thirsted for God as an exhausted deer pants for water. David was after the Father-heart of God.

In this book I have shared the stories of those who have had life-transforming encounters with Father's unending love. These individuals were either at points of desperation in their lives for more of God, or their hunger-levels were extremely high. Nonetheless, after these encounters, their lives were never the same and their ministries have transformed scores of lives and nations.

In the gospel narratives, one can read an interesting side-story which can help illustrate the importance of desire over knowledge. When they saw the star, wise men from the East came to worship the newborn Savior. They were able to locate Him because they acquired the necessary information from reading the Scriptures. King Herod knew about the expedition, so he made inquiries regarding the King of the Jews.

After realizing the method used by the Magi, King Herod instructed a coterie of Bible scholars to do the same, and, surprisingly, they were also able to pinpoint the birthplace

We must express the real reason we want to be immersed in our Father's love. We have to prove there is no ulterior motive other than having an eternal relationship with Daddy God.

of the Messiah. Yet they remained in the palace – in their comfort zone – while the Magi braved the peril of long-distance travel and the unknown just so they could worship. Both groups of men laid hold of the same information, but only one group acted on it. Desire that leads to action reveals the real motivations of the heart.

We must express the real reason we want to be immersed in our Father's love. We have to prove there is no ulterior motive other than having an eternal relationship with Daddy God. We can never receive the *Baptism of Love* if we treat it as a tool—a means to an end. If we are interested in it merely as a power source, then we will never receive it. We must simply desire the Father-heart of God. Only when we step into its center can we be baptized in His love. It is a place where deep calls unto deep, and where our longing for God collides with His affection towards us.

Jesus Longed for the Heart of His Father

Knowledge is the foundation; it is the starting point. Desire is the activator; it propels us to act on what we know. Attitude, on the other hand, sustains the action. We keep on moving forward no matter what happens. But make no mistake; we are not talking about a positivism attitude, well known in the world of men. It is not the "gung-ho" mentality exemplified by champion athletes, successful businessmen, or radical activists. When we talk about having the right attitude, we are talking about the mind-set epitomized by the

Son of God. He is our guide. He is our example.

When Jesus was only twelve years old, He demonstrated to us how one with knowledge, godly desire, and a right attitude can converge to produce a character both pleasing to Father, and able to attract heaven towards earth. When Jesus was still a child, He knew more about the Bible than the average person in Israel. At the Feast of the Passover, the twelve-year-old, Jesus, sat in the company of teachers listening and asking questions. He did not only imbibe knowledge. His righteousness exceeded that of the hard-core Pharisees because He longed for the Father-heart of God. The more He knew, the hungrier He became. The more He pursued the more He was convinced He was in the very presence of His Daddy God.

During that particular time, Jesus forgot the meaning of breakfast, lunch, and dinner. It took three long days for Mary and Joseph to locate Him. He longed to know more, and He dug deeper by asking penetrating questions. The teachers of the Law were amazed at the young boy, Jesus. At a tender age, He was quick to do away with childish things. However, these were just preliminaries. It was how Jesus dealt with frustration when His innermost desire was not realized, but revealed the hallmark of a true son.

We have to realize that the young Jesus was ready to fulfill His destiny. Just like the young Samuel many centuries before Him, Jesus was ready to live among the priests in the temple compound. He wanted to be close to the Ark of God's Presence. He longed to meditate daily on God's Word, and in turn, teach others how to find their way home to their Father. However, after three days of spiritual bliss, He was greatly disappointed when His earthly parents, Mary and Joseph, barged in and pulled Him out of the class.

Jesus had done nothing wrong. He was born to preach and teach in the temple courts. It was His destiny. Perplexed, He asked, *"Why did you seek me? Did you not know that I must be about my Father's business?"* (Luke 2:49-50, NKJV) He could have insisted, and He could have argued even further, but I believe He heard the voice of His Father in heaven. What happened next is recorded to show Jesus' desire to please the Father through His obedience to His earthly parents, *"Then He went down with them and came to Nazareth, and was subject to them [...] And Jesus increased in wisdom and stature, and in favor with God and men."* (Luke 2:51-52, NIV) This is what we call attitude. The mentality of a true son was in Jesus Christ, for just by abiding in God's Presence, hearing His voice, and obeying, Jesus was able to attract heaven towards earth.

The Finale

The next eighteen long years of obscurity, far from the object of His Father's love, was like an eternity in exile. Jesus spent almost two decades of selfless labor doing mundane tasks—fixing tables, repairing leaking roofs, re-attaching unhinged doors, and mending broken windows. He became a carpenter. It was a stark contrast to the life of a rabbi. The Old Testament was never far from His reach, but He was content to spend more time with a hammer, a measuring tape, and woodcutting instruments. This was enduring passion.

When nothing seemed to be going His way, Jesus continued the quest until finally it was time, and He knew it was the year for the Lord's favor to be released upon the earth. The promise was fulfilled because He was willing to x wait for it. He was willing to abide in the Presence of God even though nothing significant was happening to His life and ministry. In fact, for eighteen long years, Jesus had no ministry. It must have been very frustrating knowing it was His purpose in life to preach and teach, but not being able to fulfill that purpose. Yet, He endured. This is what we mean by having the right mind-set—knowledge, desire, and attitude, in perfect accord with His Father, to produce a spiritual climate conducive for the habitation of Holy Spirit.

Are we ready to embark on a journey that will change our lives, our families, our community, and the nations of the world? Are we ready to go through the process – the acquisition of godly knowledge, the purification of our desires, and the attribution of the spirit of Sonship—so Christ will be formed in us?

Jesus went through the process, even though it required,

more or less, two decades of His life. He paid the price because He saw the need. Let us pray that we may have the same Christ-like attitude. If we know how to abide and wait for the outpouring of our Father's gifts, then we will receive all of it in due time. The *Baptism of Love* is part of our inheritance because of the sacrifice and love of the Son of God. He showed us the way to our Father. Let us follow in hot pursuit and receive the gift of God.

Epilogue

The importance of the Baptism of Love is linked to the grand scheme of things. God's plan is to conquer the whole earth through a love revolution. The Bible always talks about conquest, dominion, rulership, authority, and kingdom. In the very first chapter of the Holy Book, we can find the first command ever given. It was for Adam and Eve to have dominion over everything. This command has been misinterpreted numerous times. There are times when church leaders misuse this pronouncement for their own gain. But what does it really mean?

I believe that everything was created for love. If you take away love from the equation, what you'll get is nothing less than the perversion of God's original design. Yes, God's original plan prominently displays love because He is love. Nonetheless, sin came into the world, and the command to rule and reign was perverted, bringing instead slavery, exploitation, and destruction. Check your local newspaper, and you'll find the effect of love's absence.

Moreover, without an encounter with the God of love, we are driven to perform. The Apostle Peter is the best example of a performance-oriented follower of Christ. Yet his desire to follow could not be sustained. Performance requires power, but power is not the only thing we need in life and ministry. Peter was disillusioned by lack of power, especially on the night of the crucifixion when, to him, Jesus appeared weak.

Peter was not the first person to be confused in regard to the mission plan of God on this earth. John the Baptist was on the same hallowed ground as Jesus when he baptized Him in the Jordan River and heard the same voice that said, *"This is my Son, whom I love; with Him I am well pleased."* (Matthew 3:17) Yet John the Baptist did not expect such tender words. We need to understand that before Jesus revealed Himself, John was busy preaching a message of judgment. He was passionate in reiterating, *"The ax is already at the root of the trees"*, and we can just imagine how terrifying his message sounded to his listeners.

As a forerunner and primary messenger, John the Baptist expected God to back him up in regard to his pronouncement. Instead, he was given a front-row seat to witness an affectionate moment between the Father and His Son. John the Baptist did not get the message of love. He also did not understand why Jesus spent a great deal of His time talking and eating with the worst sinners and the foremost public enemies, the tax collectors.

> *We, too, need our Father's embrace, just as Jesus did when He received His Baptism of Love. All we need to do is abide in Christ...*

Sometime later John could no longer remain silent and sent emissaries to ask Jesus, *"Are you the one who was to come, or should we expect someone else?"* (Luke 7:20, NIV) John did not yet realize that Jesus operated out of love, not from a rulebook or a merit system.

We, too, need our Father's embrace, just as Jesus did when He received His *Baptism of Love.* However, we need not stand in the Jordan River to know our Father's embrace. All we need to do is abide in Christ, for He is the Vine and we are the branches. Father is the vinedresser, and every time He dotes on His Son, every time He embraces His Son, we share in whatever emotion and blessing His Son receives from His Father. What is true of Jesus is true of us, because we are hidden in Christ. We did not make up these assertions; the Son of God Himself revealed the same to us. Listen to His unveiling:

> *"I am the way and the truth and the life. No one comes to the Father except through me. If you really knew me, you would know my Father as well. From now on, you do know him and have seen him [...]*
>
> *Anyone who has seen me has seen the Father. How can you say, 'Show us the Father'? Don't you believe that I am in the Father, and that the Father is in me? The words I say to you are not just my own. Rather, it is the Father, living in me, who is doing his work."*
>
> John 15:9-16, NIV

We are hidden in Christ Jesus while our Father is living in Him. If that is not intimacy, then I don't know what is. We are much closer to our Father than we'll ever know. If we only know who we are in Christ, then nothing will be impossible for us. Although we have to wait patiently for the outpouring of His love, we must not tarry because the whole of creation eagerly awaits the inauguration of the sons and daughters of God (see Romans 8:19). Let the love revolution begin!

About the Author

Leif Hetland is from the small town of Haugesund, Norway. In 1984 Father God took a prodigal son and restored him to his destiny. Holy Spirit transformed a broken drug addict to become a world changer that is addicted to Jesus. Leif married his wife, Jennifer, in 1989 and they are blessed with four beautiful children.

Leif is the Founder and President of Global Mission Awareness, as well as Leif Hetland Ministries. Through 28 years of ministry in 76 nations, Leif is known as an "Ambassador of Love" and is a spiritual father to an apostolic network of churches, ministries, and missionaries.

The present move of God has brought Leif into relationships with people like Randy Clark, Bill Johnson, Jack Taylor, Heidi Baker, Dr. RT Kendall, and many more. Father God has given Leif favor with God and man. Learning to be sensitive to Holy Spirit, he sees in the western world signs, wonders, and miracles that a few years ago were only being experienced in third world nations. Leif has also been used to spread the "Mission Virus" and impart power evangelism as a natural outpouring of God's Spirit on His people.

Through Global Mission Awareness and Leif Hetland Ministries Leif has authored 6 books, and speaks in conferences approximately 100 days within the western world, and 85 days in third world nations. Leif's heart is to develop a Kingdom Culture in every community that will BRING HEAVEN TO EARTH!

Leif has been through many tragic crisis in life and many of his messages have been birthed from his wilderness experiences. Leif believes in impartation and believes you "Teach what you know, but reproduce who you are!"

Some of his messages known throughout the world are Which Chair Are You Sitting In?, Healing The Orphan Spirit, Soaring As Eagles, and A Kingdom World View.

The focus of Leif is to be a spiritual son and Jack Taylor has been fathering Leif with a Spirit of Elijah so that Leif can father a Generation of Elishas for the END TIME HARVEST! His greatest joy in ministry is to see an army of sons and daughters with a great anointing and authority that are changing the course of history.

Four new messages just released
by Leif Hetland:

America: A Molting Eagle

Loving Muslims on Purpose

An Invitation to Influence Your World

Stewarding the Supernatural

Find these and other materials to bless your life at:

www.globalmissionawareness.com

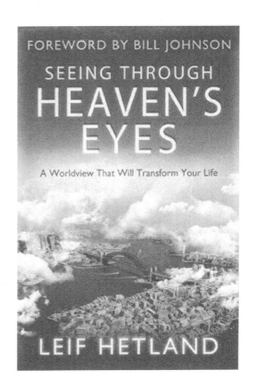

A worldview that will tranform you life!

This beautifully written memoir-essay explores the realities of Papa God's love for you, your identity as His beloved child and heir, and the transformation of your vision of yourself, others, and world events that this revelation of your place in the divine family brings.

What others are saying:

"Leif's book is profound! The very moment you shift to seeing from a heavenly perspective, everything changes!" -Lance Wallnau

"Leif is a passionate lover of Jesus Christ and his passion as an evangelist is an inspiration for all of us. It is a privilege to recommend this book." - Heidi Baker

"Like a skilled physician, Leif diagnoses the disease of humanity and prescribes the perfect cure. Leif's words will kiss you into the next realm. I highly recommend this book to anyone hungry for more of Heaven." - Kris Vallotton

Order a copy for you and your loved ones at
www.globalmissionawareness.com

Read Leif's other books:

Seeing Through Heaven's Eyes
Soaring As Eagles
28 Days of Soaring Devotional
Healing the Orphan Spirit
Soaking in God's Presence

www.globalmissionawareness.com

PO Box 3049
Peachtree City, GA 30269
770-487-4800